BLACK HOMESTEADERS

of

THE SOUTH

BLACK HOMESTEADERS

of

THE SOUTH

BERNICE ALEXANDER BENNETT

THE
History
PRESS

Published by The History Press
Charleston, SC
www.historypress.com

Family barn. *Provided by Margo Lee Williams.*

First published 2022

Manufactured in the United States

ISBN 9781467152303

Library of Congress Control Number: 2022939471

This book is dedicated to the Black men and women who toiled from sunup to sundown to live the American dream by acquiring land under the Homestead Act of 1862.

CONTENTS

CONTENTS

FOREWORD

As a descendant of a homesteader, I would like to say a few words about owning land under the Homestead Act of 1862 and the need for descendants to share their stories.

From my experience as a professional genealogist for over thirty years, I know it is so important to set a trend of listening to the family stories, sharing the oral histories and asking questions that come down the generations. As a child, I always remember how each summer, my family prepared for a vacation in Michigan. Well, it wasn't a vacation, now that I think of it. We did leave the city and head to the country. All five of us kids were excited to be on a farm—yes, a real working farm. On the farm, there was a barn, cows, work horses, chicken coops and gardens. My four brothers and I were assigned chores, which we did aside from running around and climbing trees. I had the chore of gathering eggs and feeding the chickens. There was no talk about the property being homestead property, and I had no idea of what that meant as a young child. It was just family property of where my family went every summer. *Homestead* wasn't a term I was familiar with, but the story of my family and the oral history was amazing and intriguing.

Once I had gained experience researching our family's genealogy, I began asking my mother questions regarding the family property. I wondered if she knew of any Black people who owned property or if our family rented their farm. I wanted to understand how our family became Black homesteaders as free people. I learned through oral history that we were spending our summer vacations on homestead property. This was the time for me to hit the books to study about the Homestead Act and learn about what that meant.

Finally learning about the 1862 Homestead Act helped me understand what this meant to individuals and families. Men and women could obtain 160 acres for free after fulfilling the guidelines set forth by the federal government. They had to apply and work the land by putting up a house, barn and more within five years to receive a certificate/land patent. I thought, "Wow! The 160 acres of land my family owned allowed me to play and walk on the grounds of my ancestors." I stand proud today as a Black descendant of several homesteaders.

This book will share a collection of Black homesteader stories from the South. These stories are of the families who may have been formerly enslaved—or free—and lived the American dream of being a landowner. The information shared in this book will inspire you to gather oral histories and other documents to verify that your ancestors were also homesteaders.

—Dr. Shelley Viola Murphy
(also known as "familytreegirl")

ACKNOWLEDGEMENTS

This book would not have been possible without the support of Dennis Michael Edelin, chief archivist I of the Research Room Archival Operations at the National Archives in Washington, D.C., and Jessica Korgie, park guide for the Homestead National Historical Park in Beatrice, Nebraska. Mr. Edelin supported descendants by obtaining the homestead land entry papers during a difficult period, when access to these records was impossible due to the COVID-19 pandemic. Jessica Korgie worked tirelessly to publish the Black homesteader stories on the Homestead National Park Service's (NPS) website. In addition, Amber Kirkendall, park ranger I and volunteer coordinator of Homestead National Historical Park, successfully mobilized a group of volunteers to transcribe the homestead land entry papers for their website.

I would like to acknowledge my husband, Glen Bennett, for his ongoing support of this project and my sister Janice A. Woods. In addition, I would like to say a special thanks to Denise Griggs for her expertise in editing and formatting this manuscript. Finally, Ric Murphy provided invaluable support and encouragement.

The descendants of Black homesteaders are recognized for their dedication in telling the stories of their ancestors. As family historians and genealogists, these descendants studied the homestead land entry papers, census records, gathered oral histories and used personal knowledge to write and share their stories. I applaud them and encourage others to follow in their footsteps.

The descendants and contributors to this book are acknowledged by each state.

ALABAMA

Dr. Mary K. Clark, Lyle Gibson, Orice Jenkins, Marcia Green Lamar and Charles E. Wilson.

ARKANSAS

Lyle Gibson, Susan Lasley, Jessica Trotter and Angela Walton-Raji.

FLORIDA

Falan Goff, Orice Jenkins, Deborah Mitchell and Margo Lee Williams.

LOUISIANA

Bernice A. Bennett, Alvin Blakes, Jackie M.B. Chapman, Claretha Day, Dr. Delores Mercedes Franklin, Lyle Gibson, Dr. Antoinette Harrell, Dr. Rex Holiday, Kimberli Hornes, Caleb Ricard, Clara Robertson, Felix Scott Jr., Marilyn Stubblefield and Crystal Williams-Jackson.

MISSISSIPPI

Alvin Blakes, Jonnie Ramsey Brown, Sandra Williams Bush, Nona Edwards-Thomas MD, Denise Griggs, Norma B. Hall, Dr. Antoinette Harrell, Eric Williams, Gordon Williams family and Luanne Wills-Merrell.

INTRODUCTION

*B*lack *Homesteaders of the South* tells stories of resilience and celebrates individuals, some of whom were formerly enslaved but were able, after their emancipation, to obtain up to 160 acres of public land under the Homestead Act of 1862.

The Homestead Act of 1862 was signed by President Abraham Lincoln on May 20, 1862. It went into effect on July 4, 1863.[1] The Homestead Act had two main goals: to assist the government in selling off its land to ordinary citizens and to use the land in what the government considered to be an economically efficient manner.

Therefore, the descendants of *Black Homesteaders of the South* tell the untold stories that must be revealed.

The Homestead National Historical Park Service began publishing Black homesteader stories on its website about the Black homesteaders of the Great Plains. This was a project spearheaded by the University of Nebraska–Lincoln, Nebraska Center for the Great Plains Studies for the Black homestead communities of Montana, North Dakota, South Dakota, Wyoming, Colorado, Nebraska, Kansas and New Mexico. The Black Homesteader Project, as it is called, expanded the storytelling from the Great Plains to all eligible states, aside from the thirteen original colonies and Texas. This led to an outreach effort to find other stories.

Bernice A. Bennett, a genealogist and descendant of a Black homesteader, found her ancestor's land. She led the effort to target Black family historians and genealogists in several social media spaces to join the newly created

Descendants of African American Homesteaders Facebook page. Through this page, individuals are provided with the basic steps to find their landowning ancestors through research at the Bureau of Land Management's website. With this information, they are encouraged to order their land entry papers from the National Archives and Records Administration and are given a template with which to write and tell their stories.

Many stories from the South emerged from this grassroots process and identified Black settlers who acquired land as early as 1872 and as late as 1930. In addition, these stories populated the NPS website with new information about individuals from Alabama, Arkansas, Louisiana, Florida and Mississippi.

The stories in this book are from the descendants and genealogists who researched the process and celebrated their ancestors' accomplishments. For many, learning about the Homestead Act of 1862 provided new information and concrete documentation that their ancestors took the brave step to apply for and receive a land patent or deed.[2] The documentation from the homestead land entry papers added dates and vital information regarding the location of the land, the age and birthplace of the claimant/applicant, the original date they settled on the land, the number of family members living on the land, improvements made and the identities and testimonies of witnesses.

Further research through other sources also revealed that some of the applicants were born enslaved, were members of the United States Colored Troops or were parts of communities of Black landowners. In addition, these case files could reveal that the settler already owned land and that they were adding to their adjacent property.

This book will bring to light the journey of forty-nine Black homesteaders of the South in the rural communities of Alabama, Arkansas, Florida, Louisiana and Mississippi. These individuals persevered to live the American dream to become landowning farmers. Their stories have never been told.

This is the first book of its kind, in which the descendants tell how their ancestors met the eligibility requirements to apply for and obtain this homesteaded land. Those guidelines stipulated that the individual had to: be a citizen or have the intent to become a citizen (meaning immigrants could apply for this land); not have borne arms against the United States; be the head of household; be a widow, single male or female, formerly enslaved and over the age of twenty-one; not have already owned 160 acres or more; and live on and improve the land for a minimum of five years.

This task was not easy, as most applicants had to have money to apply for the land (filing fees) and funds to purchase farm tools, along with other resources for cultivation. They also needed community support from their family and friends to assist with this process.

Owning land in the rural South represented the opportunity that formerly enslaved individuals desired. As descendants of homesteaders, we view this as the ultimate freedom—to live in their own home and on their own land.

As descendants, we are following in the footsteps of other Black family historians/genealogists and storytellers who have written about the homesteading experiences of their ancestors.

Thomas W. Mitchell, in his scholarly article "Destabilizing the Normalization of Rural Black Land Loss," mentioned how films and even TV shows have made white homesteaders' stories part of the folk history, while Black homesteaders of the rural South have been ignored.

Historian, Nell Irvin Painter provides an excellent historical perspective about the thousands of Black citizens who fled the South to obtain homesteaded land in Kansas. While this moment in American history about the Black Exodusters is well documented, we are finding through our research that many Black Americans remained in the rural South and some did acquire land there. However, additional research should be encouraged, and those stories must be told.

This book is a call to action to inspire and influence others to look for the stories of Black homesteaders in the rural South and around the country and to share them.

1

ALABAMA BLACK HOMESTEADERS

Every generation leaves behind a legacy. What that legacy is will be determined by the people of that generation. What legacy do you want to leave behind?
—Representative John Lewis; Troy, Alabama

About 4.5 million acres—out of the state's total land area of 33.5 million acres—of homesteaded land were available to Americans in Alabama. In the end, 41,819 homestead applications were filed and proved. Five out of the six Homesteaders in this chapter lived in counties in the southeastern corner of Alabama. Each of these counties suffered severe courthouse fires between the Civil War and the start of the twentieth century, destroying many marriage, probate and property records. The importance of federal records was exemplified so clearly upon reading homestead entry papers from this area. Even federal records, such as the 1890 United States census, are missing from this crucial period that followed Reconstruction. As Black Alabamians struggled to dig themselves out of bondage, the documentation of their successes was buried even further, and the unearthing of their homestead files in 2022 is invaluably critical to understanding the lives of these ancestors.

The Alabama Territory was formed in 1817 from the Mississippi Territory, as Mississippi was becoming a state. The capital of the Alabama Territory, St. Stephens, was used as the meridian for the location markers of these homestead lands. St. Stephens is now an unincorporated community just sixty-seven miles north of Mobile, Alabama. Across the state is Dale County, which was formed in 1825 and later became the parent county to Coffee and Geneva Counties. After speaking with family members and other homestead descendants, Orice Jenkins, a descendant of a homesteader, was able to identify twenty-five other Black homesteaders in southeast Alabama, with some of the land being marked by the Tallahassee Meridian. Geneva County is bordered by Florida. Therefore, Orice found homesteaders from the same families across the state line. Over 3,640 acres of land were patented to the Black Americans listed in this chapter.

LUKE SCONIERS

By Charles E. Wilson

The first generation of Sconiers began with Luke's father, Solomon Sconyers, and his uncle King Dock Sconyers, another homesteader.[3] Solomon met his partner, Liddie, in Dale County, Alabama, and they bore a son, Luke.[4] Luke was most likely born in 1854, according to census records.[5] Records indicate that Solomon and Dock were together as enslaved persons with their slaveholder, Allen Sconyers, in 1850 and 1860.[6] Consequently, Luke Sconiers was born as one of Allen Sconyers's slaves in Clayhatchee, Alabama.

Solomon and Dock remained in Dale County, Alabama, at the time of emancipation. They became registered voters in the State of Alabama in 1867.[7] It had to be a proud moment, as Luke may have witnessed his father, Solomon, and his uncle King Dock register to vote as emancipated men, the privilege already afforded to their former slaveholder and former slave holder's son.[8]

Luke was approximately sixteen years of age in 1870.[9] Once enslaved and now emancipated, Luke lived with his father, Solomon, and stepmother, Mendy, in Geneva County. His siblings, Phyllis and James, were also listed as part of the household unit. Luke was married to Ellen Louisa Engram in 1873, when Ellen was just seventeen.[10]

On January 24, 1879, Luke filed Homestead Application no. 8157 at the circuit court in Geneva County. By 1880, Luke and Ellen had five children: James Bartlett, Aaron Rasberry, Reuben H., Charlotte Victoria "Lottie" and Daniel. Luke was a farmer by occupation, while Ellen maintained the home of what was to be the start of a large Sconiers household.[11] The 1880 property, in which they resided, became the watershed of Luke and his wife, Ellen, who owned land as an emancipated Black family.

Luke made his final affidavit on March 22, 1884, stating that he settled on his land in 1875. According to his testimony on the claimant form, he built a log dwelling and a meat house and cleared thirty acres of land. By this point, he and Ellen had seven children. Witness testimonies were given by their neighbor Bedford Donnell and Ellen's father, James Engram. Luke Sconiers received his land patent from the United States government, signed by President Grover Cleveland on March 30, 1885, twenty years after emancipation. This land patent granted him full private ownership of the land he had resided on since 1875.[12]

Although Luke could not read or write, the importance of him being presented with a certificate signed by the president of the United States had a lasting impression on him and his family. By 1885, Luke Sconiers owned one-fourth of a square mile or 160.33 acres of land without any mortgage obligation. To put this in perspective, the area would be the size of 160 football fields.[13] This became the home of the family's seventeen children by the 1900s. Luke went on to purchase 240 more acres of land between 1886 and 1895.[14]

Luke and Ellen, inspired by the movement of the African Methodist Episcopal Church (AME), moved on to philanthropic interests. They donated land for building a church named after the wife of Luke's uncle Dock, the Mount Mariah African Methodist Episcopal Church.[15] The period marked a possible change in the spelling of their surname from Sconyers to Sconiers. Although the surnames Sconyers and Sconiers were used interchangeably, most Black Sconyers/Sconiers make use of the spelling Sconiers.[16]

At any given time, seventeen children were living on the land that was owned by Luke, and by 1900, twelve were living on the land.[17] Luke and Ellen lived to see seven of their children precede them in death: James, Reuben, Ely, David, Mollie, Dick and Nealie. Reuben died around 1909.[18] On the land that Luke owned, both Ellen and Luke were involved in the lives of their children, providing care to the community around them and to Luke's father, Solomon.[19]

The year 1910 marked forty-five years since emancipation. Luke, at the age of sixty-two, remained on his property as its owner without any mortgage debt. His wife, Ellen, was fifty-four years old and had been married to Luke for over thirty-seven years.[20] On September 29, 1910, Luke and Ellen gave land to the Masons of Bellwood Star Lodge no. 269.[21] Luke's father, Solomon, was living with Ellen and Luke until his death in 1911.[22]

On April 21, 1915, Ellen was approaching sixty years of age and had completed her last will and testament. Luke and one of his sons, King

Sconyers, were named as the executors of Ellen's last will and testament.[23] Three years later, after the will was written, Ellen was approaching the age of sixty-three. Ellen died on May 21, 1918, fifty-three years after emancipation.[24] There were no other records of her death or burial discovered.

Luke was a widower after many years of marriage with Ellen. The losses Luke experienced with the death of his son Reuben in 1909; his father, Solomon, in 1911; and his wife, Ellen, in 1918 had to have taken a toll on his health.[25] Luke emphatically declared after Ellen's death that he had a desire to have one of his children, King Sconyers, be the sole executor of the last will and testament of Ellen and to carry out all the responsibilities, since he was too old and infirmed to continue to do such things.[26] Two years after Ellen's death, Luke died, on April 20, 1920.[27] His death certificate is one of the few vital and public records of Luke available; it did not include the identity of the informant or the recorder or where Luke was buried.

Luke was born enslaved, lived through emancipation, was registered as a voter, owned land during Reconstruction in the South and used his freedom to become a homesteader. Because of his tenacity, the Sconiers family still owned their land as of 2021. Mount Mariah AME Church no longer stands, but its cemetery remains in use, now known as Mount Mariah Memorial Cemetery.

CONTRIBUTOR: *Charles Wilson is a retired U.S. Navy chaplain and sole proprietor of the Wilson Griot Legacy. His wife, Burlenda, and daughters, Charla and Bonita, are direct descendants of Luke and Ellen Sconiers.*

WILLIAM BEARD

By Marcia Green Lamar

I discovered the homestead land patent on Ancestry.com when I was researching my Beard/Moffett family history. Until that time, I had no idea how the Beard family had come into owning so much land. William Beard was born enslaved in Leaksville, Mississippi, on January 14, 1854. He was one of three children—two boys and a girl—who were born to Joe Beard and Sarah (McKinnis) Beard. In the 1870 U.S. census, he and his siblings were recorded as living with their grandmother Hannah Polk in Jackson County, Mississippi.[28] Shortly after that time, William married Ann Moffett

William Beard. *Courtesy of Marcia Green Lamar.*

William's wife, Cynthia. *Courtesy of Marcia Green Lamar.*

and went to live in Wilmer, Mobile, Alabama. In the 1880 census, his occupation is listed as a worker in the timber industry, and he and his wife had four children (Joseph, William, E. John and Ellen). William and Ann Moffett had seven children before her death in 1885.[29]

William submitted Homestead Application no. 714 on November 21, 1877. He built a house and fence and cultivated about six acres of land. In addition, he also built a stable, a corncrib and other outhouses. He eventually farmed a large amount of the land, where the family was able to grow a variety of fruits and vegetables. In addition, he also raised animals and had a smokehouse for storing meat. The Beard family was never hungry and was able to share food with other families when they were in need. Although William Beard could read and write, he used an X as his signature on his land entry document.

William Beard had the following witnesses testify to support his final homestead claim: Jackson Moffett, the brother of his wife, Ann Moffett; and Wesley Taylor, a neighbor. Williams's brother-in-law Jackson testified on the homestead land application that William settled in Wilmer/Moffettville, Alabama, on September 4, 1871. The final homestead application was submitted on November 21, 1877, for 159.98 acres of land. William received Homestead Land Patent no. 364 on December 30, 1879.

In addition to farming the land, William was a logger by trade. His last living daughter, my great-aunt Eleonore, provided an account of some of his life during that time. She said that her father was a straw boss in the logging business, which meant that he had to supervise the workers and count and document the logs that were shipped to other merchants. He also harvested logs and took them up and down the river. He had a logging team in Alabama and Mississippi. Because he was unable to personally supervise this team in Mississippi, he lost a large sum of money and had to close the business there. However, the business in Alabama was profitable and employed family members and others in the community.

William was a Christian by faith. His in-laws (Cyrus John Moffett and Rachel Banks Moffett) founded the Moffettville Baptist Church on Wilson Road in December 1868 and later organized it in August 1876. He served as chairman of the deacon board and was actively involved in his community, offering counseling and support to people to uphold the moral standards of Christ in the Wilmer/ Moffettville community.

Upon the death of his wife, Ann, William continued to raise his children on the farm. He later married her sister Sabrie Ella in April 1889. It appears that Ann's sister was the best person to take care of the children. From this union, William had ten additional children. Sabrie Ella died in 1905. William then married Ada Bales Robinson, but she died in 1918, so he finally married Cynthia Ann Adams. Cynthia, a widow, had two sons before her marriage to William and later had a daughter.

William Beard died on May 31, 1939, and was buried in Mobile, Alabama.[30] His daughter Eleonore lived until 2013 and was able to share family information.

William's children lived on parts of the land and farmed, just as he had done. As of today, few family members still own or live on parts of this land.

Moffettville Baptist Church founders' foundation stone. *Courtesy of Marcia Green Lamar.*

The home that William built is no longer standing. After the death of his last wife, the home was vacant and later destroyed by a hurricane.

I remember going to Wilmer/Moffettville to visit relatives. We would ride horses, pick fruit off the trees and vines, eat great food and attend church, especially during homecomings. I would see many family members and clean the cemetery with my mother and grandmother. Now, my husband and I keep the tradition alive by going to the cemetery to make sure that all the graves are cleaned.

CONTRIBUTOR: *Marcia Green Lamar is a direct descendant of William Beard through his son John Enoch Beard. She is a self-taught intermediate genealogist and just one of the family historians who are researching and documenting the Beard and Moffett families' journeys.*

CLEM HORN

By Orice Jenkins

Clem Horn was born enslaved in Georgia in 1826.[31] After emancipation, he moved across the Chattahoochee River into Henry County, Alabama. He was enumerated on the 1870 census in the community of Lawrenceville with his wife, Sarah, and two of their daughters: Elizabeth and Jane. In 1873, Elizabeth (later known as Betty) married Warren Law at the historic Piney Grove Baptist Church in Headland, Alabama.[32] They were married by Reverend Jesse Grant, a Black homesteader who may have been the catalyst for Clem finding his homesteaded land.[33]

Clem became a widower and moved sixty miles southwest to Coffee County, Alabama, in the late 1870s.[34] Betty separated from her husband, relocated with her father and married a homesteader from Coffee Springs named Vandy Hutchins.[35] Clem was remarried to a young woman named Caroline McGowan and then settled less than a mile away from Vandy's farm.[36]

On August 11, 1883, Clem went to the office of Benjamin M. Stevens, the judge of probate court in Elba, Alabama. He filed Homestead Application no. 14524 for 160.4 acres of land in Coffee County. He also filed a homestead affidavit for settlers who couldn't travel to the district land office in Montgomery. He settled on the land on January 1, 1881, and made seventy-five dollars' worth of improvements, including the construction of a one-room dwelling house and clearing 25 acres of land. He signed the document with an X, indicating that he could not read or write. Clem's application, as well as a filing fee of fourteen dollars, reached the receiver's office in Montgomery on August 15, 1883.

On October 15, 1888, Clem returned to the courthouse in Elba to make his final affidavit. He testified that the property was "ordinary pine timberland valuable only for farming." He explained that he bought the land from Stephen Stokes, who had built the sixteen-by-eighteen-foot log house that the Horn family was living in. Within the house was one bed, five chairs and one table, which Clem claimed he had owned "since freedom," confirming his former enslavement. The value of the improvements was then valued at eighty-five dollars, including the construction of a smokehouse that was worth ten dollars. Clem also owned an ox, a plow and five head of cattle. Clem raised twenty acres of crops, such as corn and cotton, in 1888. He stated that he had cultivated up to twenty-five acres of produce in the past.

Clem's family at that time consisted of his wife, Caroline, and their five children, but they went on to have twelve children together.[37] Clem said he had never voted before, citing his status as an "old negro" as the only reason for this. Clem signed his affidavit with his name instead of an X, showing that he had learned to write by 1888.

His witnesses were two young men: Caroline's brother William McGowan and Green Thompson. Green testified that Clem's land was worth $1.25 per acre, while William claimed it was worth $1.50 per acre. Both men lived a half mile away from Clem's homestead and listed a white man named Abraham Chancellor as another close neighbor. The unincorporated community of Chancellor, Alabama, was named after Abraham's father.[38]

On November 13, 1888, the land office in Montgomery received Clem's final payment of four dollars and issued him certificate no. 7508, proclaiming that he was entitled to a land patent for the southern half of the northwest quarter and the northern half of the southwest quarter of

A signature. *Illustration by Edward LaRose.*

section 28 in township 3 north of range 22 east. The southern perimeter of section 28 is the Coffee/Geneva County line. Clem's land is currently bordered to the north by County Road 732 and to the east by Thomas Road in Chancellor, Alabama. The patent was signed by President Benjamin Harrison on June 8, 1891, over ten years after Clem made his settlement.

A deed was recorded on September 11, 1891, that shows Coffee County constable Leonidas "Lee" Bray and his wife, Rebecca, selling Clem's land to Jefferson Cutts for $525.[39] While this deed was filed three months after Clem's patent was issued, it is dated November 26, 1890, eight months before the patent date. Probate Judge Benjamin M. Stevens recorded the deed in the same barely legible handwriting that he used to record Clem's homestead application and homestead affidavits several years earlier.

The timing of the deed is peculiar, as Clem's settlement on the property was publicized in the *Coffee County News* for six weeks starting in September 1888 to determine if there were other claimants to the land. Regardless, Clem was no longer the legal owner of the farm, and it was continuously referred to as the "Jeff Cutts Plantation" in subsequent deeds. Both Leonidas Bray and Jefferson Cutts had applied for their homesteads in the same area. Bray received 80.06 acres on June 19, 1891, but Cutt's patent was canceled on December 1, 1890. A deed for the land that mentions Clem Horn has not yet been found.

In the 1900 census, it appears Clem was living on the farm of William Bridges Noblin in Geneva County, Alabama. William had his homestead seventeen miles southeast of Clem's. They both received their patents in June 1891, but William Noblin was not a Black homesteader. He was able to pass his homestead lands on to his descendants and even had a census-designated place named after him.

Clem died before the 1910 census in Noblin, Alabama. His widow, Caroline, moved ninety miles west to Castleberry, Alabama, where she died on December 15, 1944.[40] She was the daughter of a homesteader named Lucy McGowan, and her family members still own property in Coffee County as of 2021. Clem fathered at least fourteen children with Sarah and Caroline between 1850 and 1899, many of whom spread throughout the Wiregrass region of Georgia, Florida and Alabama.

CONTRIBUTOR: *Orice Jenkins is the great-great-great-grandson of Clem and Sarah Horn. He is a recording artist, genealogist and educator.*

VANDY HUTCHINS

By Orice Jenkins

Vandy Hutchins was born enslaved in Coffee County, Alabama, in the early 1850s.[41] His descendants use various spellings of their surname, including Hutchinson and Hutchison. My grandmother chose Hutchison but did not know anything about Vandy's family, even though she lived near him in Georgia. She didn't know that he came from Alabama or that he was a landowner. I discovered his land patent on Ancestry.com, which prompted me to request his original application. On November 13, 1883, Vandy filed Homestead Application no. 15029 for 160.11 acres of land in Geneva County, which had been formed out of the southern part of Coffee County in 1868.

Vandy was not able to report to the district land office in Montgomery to make his homestead affidavit due to its "great distance" from his home. It was instead signed before Sidney Franklin Latimer, the clerk of court for Geneva County, at the courthouse in the city of Geneva on November 13, 1883. Vandy could not read or write, so he signed with an X. He testified in the affidavit that he had settled on the land in January 1879, which was edited to 1880. He also stated that he had built a log house and cleared one acre of land so far, all worth fifteen dollars. Vandy's application, affidavit and a filing fee of fourteen dollars reached the receiver's office in Montgomery on November 17, 1883.

Five years later, on December 21, 1888, Vandy returned to the courthouse in Geneva to swear to his improvement of the land. He testified that the tract was nothing more than "common piney woods farming land." This time, he stated that he had settled on the land in the fall of 1882. He said that he was never absent from his land once he settled on it and that he voted at beat no. 10 in Geneva County. His family consisted of his wife, the former Elizabeth "Betty" Horn, and four children: Henry, Almaria, Clem and Tyson.[42] Betty was most likely pregnant with their daughter Daisy at this time, who was followed by Arnold, or "Ornt," in 1890 and Cora in 1892.[43] Betty also had a thirteen-year-old daughter named Ella from her previous marriage to Warren Law.[44]

Vandy reported that he owned one plow, one hoe, two axes, two beds, three chairs and one table but no livestock. He had then cleared six acres of land to raise corn and cotton crops, but he did not know how much he had produced when he was asked. Witness testimonies were given by Green Thompson and Edward "Ned" Bryant, Green's father-in-law. Green and Ned's testimonies are nearly identical, naming two of Vandy's neighbors, John Talley and Christopher Thurman; giving the dimensions of his log house as fourteen by twelve feet; valuing his land at $200; and claiming they saw Vandy on the land the night before. All three testimonies differ on the value of the house. Vandy was modest, claiming his house was worth just ten dollars, while Ned and Green valued it at fifteen and twenty dollars, respectively.

On December 27, 1888, the land office in Montgomery received Vandy's final payment of four dollars and issued him certificate no. 7657, proclaiming that he was entitled to a patent for the eastern half of the northwest quarter and the northern half of the northeast quarter of section 33 in township 3 north of range 22 east. Vandy's land was bounded by the current Coffee/Geneva County line. Lake Fox Road in Chancellor, Alabama, runs through the land today. The patent was signed by President Benjamin Harrison on June 8, 1891. At this point, Vandy may have already been living on the land for twelve years.

By 1896, Vandy was not living on his homestead anymore.[45] In 1898, the county courthouse in Geneva suffered a destructive fire, burning any government record that existed saying Vandy sold or lost his land. The earliest surviving deed is from February 10, 1902, when a wealthy merchant and banker named James Jefferson Johnson sold half of the homestead for $200.[46] Vandy may have willingly sold his homestead to this man between 1891 and 1896, but it should be noted that Johnson was the son-in-law of Sidney Franklin Latimer, the clerk of court who processed Vandy's homestead application.[47] Johnson later became the president of the Citizens Bank in Geneva and had considerable influence throughout the county.[48] He sold 80 acres of Vandy's farm to John Duncan Wilson, a wealthy homesteader who eventually owned all of Vandy's land and much of the surrounding property, totaling 907 acres.

Wilson mortgaged the property for $18,000 in 1924 to the Federal Land Bank of New Orleans. The mortgage was foreclosed on in 1931, and the land was put up for auction at the Coffee County Courthouse in Enterprise, Alabama. The highest bid of $7,375 was made by the Federal Land Bank of New Orleans. It sold the land to the Alabama Rural Rehabilitation Corporation in 1935, which sold it two years later to its original non-Native owner, the United States of America. At this point, the land was known as Coffee Farms, a project of the Farm Security Administration. A 217-acre portion of Coffee Farms that included Vandy's homestead was finally purchased by a Black couple named Benjamin and Candis McCray in 1943 for $3,200. Their family still owned some of the lands as of 2021.[49]

Meanwhile, Vandy and his family ended up sixty miles to the east in the Urquhart district of Early County, Georgia. He registered to vote there in 1897, swearing that he had lived in Georgia for at least one year.[50] Betty's former residence of Lawrenceville, Alabama, was located in the neighboring Henry County, just over the Chattahoochee River, which serves as the state's border. Vandy and Betty spent the rest of their lives working on the Sawyer-King Farm on Grimsley Mill Road.[51] The farm's owner, Oswald King, fathered the child of Cora Hutchins, Vandy's daughter. Vandy and Betty raised their biracial grandson after Cora's premature death, never returning to Alabama or sharing their homesteading story with their descendants. Betty died on June 1, 1931, and Vandy died on November 29 of the same year.[52] It has not yet been discovered why they didn't hold on to their homestead, but their grandson was able to purchase his farm in 1975, continuing the legacy of landownership in the Hutchins family for future generations.[53]

Contributor: Orice Jenkins is the great-great-grandson of Vandy Hutchins and Betty Horn. He is a recording artist, genealogist and educator.

FRANK CRITTENDEN

By Lyle Gibson

Throughout my genealogical journey, I have used the Bureau of Land Management's website to research land patents; however, I only focused on pre-1862 records. It wasn't until 2020, when I learned of efforts to document Black homesteaders, that I began to take a closer look. In 2020, I started the process and soon discovered that different branches of my family were applicants of the 1862 Homestead Act.

Frank Crittenden, my great-great-grand uncle, who was formerly enslaved, was one of the few in my family to initiate this process. Frank Crittenden was born in July 1848 in Sumter County, Georgia, to Charles and Flaywilla Crittenden, who had eleven other children: Allie Crittenden-Gilmore, born in 1836 in Talbot County, Georgia; James "Jim" Crittenden, born in 1838 in Talbot County, Georgia, and died in May 1912 in Coffee County, Alabama; Adam Crittenden, born in 1839 in Talbot County, Georgia; Gilbert Crittenden, born in 1844 in Talbot County, Georgia, and died in January 1928 in Dale County, Alabama; Isaiah Crittenden, born in 1844 in Schley County, Georgia, and died in August 1912 in Dale County, Alabama; Adeline Crittenden, born in 1845 in Schley County, Georgia; Ammon Crittenden, born in 1846 in Schley County, Georgia, and died in 1918 in Dale County, Alabama; Lydia Crittenden, born in 1848 in Schley County, Georgia; Eliza, born in 1848 in Schley County, Georgia; Andrew Crittenden, born in 1850 in Schley County, Georgia, and died in 1936 in Dale County, Alabama; and Jonas Crittenden, born in 1855 Sumter County, Georgia. Frank Crittenden, along with his father and siblings, were listed in a Freedmen's Bureau record for a labor contract with C.D. Crittenden in Dale County, Alabama, dated June 1, 1865.

Frank and his parents and siblings were enslaved to Judge Cincinattus Decatur Crittenden, the son of Robert Greene Crittenden and Nancy Mahone. Robert G. Crittenden was the son of Frederick Greene and Frances M. Crittenden. Robert's parents died when he was young, and he was raised by his uncle Robert Crittenden. Robert Crittenden's maternal grandfather was Henry Crittenden.

Frank Crittenden settled on his land located in Dale County, Alabama, on December 21, 1887, and submitted Homestead Application no. 22012 on December 4, 1888, for eighty acres of land located on section 1, township 4n, range 23 east. Per his testimony, Frank stated that he had a wife and five children and had lived on the land since 1888.

He received Homestead Patent no. 12971 on January 4, 1894, for eighty acres, of which, thirty acres were cleared for cultivation and included a "log dwelling, corn crib, and smokehouse."

Per the 1870 and 1900 Dale County, Alabama censuses, Frank's family at the time of the 1888 homestead application included him, his wife, Dicey, and their five children—Richard, born 1867; Ammie, born 1873; Etta, born 1884; Cincey, born 1885; and Erastus, born 1887.

In addition to the standard resources used to verify the lives of Frank Crittenden and his family, a Bible maintained by Judge C.D. Crittenden provided the names and birth dates of those he had enslaved. The lives of Frank and his brothers were documented in primary source documents that include newspaper accounts from the late nineteenth century in Dale County, Alabama.

Frank, his brothers and a brother-in-law, John Gilmore (the husband of Allie Crittenden), were skilled artisans, primarily working as blacksmiths. Frank's brother Jim Crittenden was a "body servant to Colonel Robert F. Crittenden during the U.S. Civil War." One brother, Adam Crittenden, moved back to Sumter County, Geogria, after the war; there, he and his family lived out their lives. Through the use of DNA technology, descendants of Allie Crittenden-Gilmore, Adam Crittenden (through his son Marshall Crittenden), Frank Crittenden and Andrew Crittenden show a genetic connection leading back to the common ancestors of Charles and Flaywilla Crittenden. Additionally, the name Flaywilla is very unusual; however, when researching names found within West African societies, it is a name that means "flower." There are two other descendants of Flaywilla Crittenden who carry this name, Flaywilla Gilmore, the daughter of Allie Crittenden-Gilmore, and Flaywilla Byrd, the granddaughter of Ammon Crittenden.

Per the homestead application, Frank signed his name with an X. The witnesses were Jackson Snipes and Judge Dean. Both Snipes and Dean concurred in their statements regarding the state of thirty acres of improved land and the presence of a dwelling house, corncrib and smokehouse.

CONTRIBUTOR: *Lyle Gibson is the great-great-grandnephew of Frank Crittenden. Gibson's great-great-grandmother Allie Crittenden-Gilmore was the sister of Frank Crittenden.*

JOHN HENRY KYLES

By Mary K. Clark, PhD

As a child, I would visit my maternal grandfather, Joe Kyles, who lived with Ma Jane, his common-law companion, in a small home in Vassar, Michigan. Every visit, I would see a sepia-toned picture that hung in the front room of his home, directly across from Joe's bed. The front room also served as his bedroom. He would sit on the elevated twin-sized bed during the day and talk with visitors as they sat on a large wood steamer trunk directly across from his bed.

In retrospect, I wish that I would have asked him who those people in the picture were. I regret not hearing any story that Grandpa Joe would have shared with me. Grandpa Joe died when I was a college freshman. Several years later, I saw that same picture in my parent's home. I asked my mother, "Who are the people in that old picture?" She replied, "That's Grandpa Joe's mother and father, Fannie and John Henry Kyles." That was my introduction to my great-grandparents John Henry and Frances "Fannie" Eddins Kyles. I would eventually learn a few more unsubstantiated details about their lives

John Henry and Frances Kyles. *Courtesy of Mary K. Clark, PhD.*

through family oral history. It is an honor to share the following facts about John Kyles and his family's experience as Alabama homesteaders.

Some oral history shared by my maternal grand-aunt Carrie Belle Kyles Weeks, the daughter of John Henry and Sarah Kyles, was that John was a farmer. She described him as "land rich." He rented a portion of his land to other farmers while he took care of his parents until their deaths. That was the extent of knowledge I had about John Henry Kyles. What follows is my version of his story based on my research.

John Kyles gained some knowledge about the homesteading process from his father's experience. Willis Kyles established residence in January 1885, submitted his homestead application on January 2, 1886, and obtained his land patent for his homestead on November 9, 1891. John was inspired to have a homestead for his own family. Research revealed variations of the Kyles surname, which include Kylis, Kyle, Kyler and Kytes. John Kyles had several name variations as well, including Henry J., John Henry, John H. and Henry. He had a brother named John C. Kyles who was about ten years older. In at least two instances on census records, John C. was recorded as living in a residence next to John Henry and his family. John C. was never a homesteader.

John Kyles filed Homestead Application no. 23027 on October 10, 1889, at the Office of the Clerk of the Court for Geneva County to settle on public land in Coffee Springs, Geneva County, Alabama. John solemnly swore that he was "a native-born citizen of the U.S. and over twenty-one years of age" and confirmed that he had resided on the land since October 29, 1888. As his father worked to clear and make improvements to the land that would later become his homestead, John also began the process of becoming a homesteader.

Kyles's application was made for actual settlement and cultivation for his exclusive use and benefit, not directly or indirectly for the use or benefit of any other person. John confirmed that his improvements included the construction of one log dwelling and one cookhouse and the clearing of seven acres of land, the cultivation of which he valued at $200. He indicated that because of the great distance to the district land office in Montgomery, he was unable to appear in person to file the homestead affidavit. He confirmed that he had never made a homestead entry and provided his mark, an X. The homestead affidavit was signed by S.F. Latimer, the clerk of the court of Geneva County, Alabama, on October 10, 1889.

On the same day, at the post office in Coffee Springs, Alabama, the application for the homestead property in Geneva County was submitted. Under section 2289, revised statutes of the United States, John Kyles submitted the application for surveyed lands located at the northern half of the southwest quarter, the northwestern quarter of the southeast quarter and the southeastern quarter of the northwest quarter of section 34 in township 3, north of range 21, east of the St. Stephens Principal Meridian containing 160.78 acres.

John's request was received and acknowledged by the land office in Montgomery, Alabama, on October 12, 1889. Julian H. Bingham, the register of the land office, certified the application for surveyed lands under the revised statutes of the United States and confirmed that the application was valid.

After the land was properly registered, the receiver's office in Montgomery acknowledged the receipt of fourteen dollars from John Kyles on October 12, 1889, as the fee and compensation for the register and receiver for the entry of property located at northern half of the southwest quarter, the northwestern quarter of the southeast quarter and the southeastern quarter of the northwest quarter of section 34 in township 3, north of range 21, east of the St. Stephens Principal Meridian. This receipt was signed by Nathan H. Alexander, Receiver.

John's desire to obtain a homestead was inspired by his intention to establish a home for his future family. On June 23, 1892, John (Henry) Kyles obtained a license to marry Frances Eddins. Their rites of matrimony were witnessed by Peter Eddins (the inferred father of Frances), and the marriage was solemnized by Hamp Thomas, a minister. The license was signed by Judge B.M. Stephens of the Coffee County Probate Court.

John continued to work hard to complete the process of obtaining his homestead. This was made known by Public Notice no. 14256 indicating John's intention to make final proof in support of his claim. This notice was posted from October 31, 1893, to December 16, 1893, in the *Geneva Mirror*, a newspaper published by the Mirror Publishing Company. The names of witnesses who could prove that John Kyles maintained continuous residence and cultivated the land were included in the posting. The witnesses' names were John T. Harrison, Henry Finney, Alexander Fitzpatrick and Archie McNair, all of Coffee Springs, Alabama. This public notice was acknowledged by J.H. Bingham, the register in Chancery Court for Geneva, Alabama.

John provided the following claimant homestead proof and testimony of claimant on December 16, 1893. He was thirty-five years old at the time, and the post office that served his area was located in Coffee Springs, Alabama. He acknowledged that he was a natural citizen, born in Mississippi, although most of the census records indicate that he was born in Georgia. He claimed to be the person who made the homestead entry on October 12, 1889. He described the land he claimed as primarily pine and timber woodland that was only fit for farming purposes.

His initial residence was established in October 1888. The improvements to the land included the construction of a log dwelling and a cookhouse and the clearing of fifty acres of open land. He placed the value of his homestead at $400. He lived continuously on the land with his wife and two children, and he had never been absent from the homestead since making the settlement.

He cultivated about fifty acres of crops each year for a total of five years. His land was not within the limits of an incorporated town or used for trade and business in any way. There were no indications of the presence of coal or minerals of any kind on the land. He had not made any other homestead entry, and he had not sold, conveyed or mortgaged any portion of his land. He did not have any personal property of any kind elsewhere. He completed the form with his full signature, not the X he used on his initial application four years earlier. His claimant testimony was certified and signed by R.M. Gray, a register on December 16, 1893.

Two witnesses provided statements in support of his application. John T. Harrison, twenty-seven years old, and Archie McNair, thirty-five years old, both confirmed everything stated by John Kyles. They both listed improvements to the land, including one log dwelling, one cookhouse and fifty acres of open land valued at $400. Both witnesses signed their respective statements with their names. Both testimonies were signed by R.M. Gray, the register in Chancery for Geneva County, Alabama, on December 16, 1893.

Three years after John's father received his land patent for 120.08 acres on November 9, 1891, John was finalizing his own homestead. In the final affidavit required of homestead claimants, John Kyles solemnly swore that he was a citizen of the United States and that he settled, cultivated and resided on the land from October 29, 1888, to December 16, 1893. He was the sole bona fide owner of the actual settlement. The affidavit was signed by John Kyles and certified by R.M. Gray, the register in Chancery for Geneva County, Alabama, on December 16, 1893.

John Kyles made the final payment of sixty cents to the Montgomery Receiver's Office on January 11, 1894. Final Certificate no. 12820 for 160.78 acres was certified at the Montgomery Land Office on the same day and signed by J.H. Bingham, register. The homestead application was approved on October 20, 1894, and was finally patented on November 21, 1894, signed by President Grover Cleveland and recorded in volume 25, page 373 of the land office records.

John Kyle's story doesn't end there. While researching, it was evident that the ages listed on the homestead and census records varied noticeably. For example, in 1893, in his claimant statement, John reported his age as thirty-five. However, in the 1900 census, his age is recorded as thirty.

There are numerous age discrepancies noted for many of his family members throughout this story. This author wanted to clarify that any incorrect ages included are not attributable to error, but they are a reflection of the information within the sources used to tell this story.

In the 1900 census, John Kyles, thirty, and his wife, Frances "Fannie," twenty-seven, were enumerated in Beaver Dam, Geneva County, Alabama. They had three children: Lula, four; Arcus, two; and Matterson, six months. Also living in the household was Kyles's widowed mother, Dollie Kyles. Neighboring homesteads included individuals who served as witnesses for Kyles's homestead application, such as Archibald McNair, John T. Harrison and Lizzie Fitzpatrick, the widow of Alexander Fitzpatrick.

By the 1910 census, John, forty-three, and Frances, thirty-eight, were enumerated on Settlement Road in Beaver Dam, Geneva County. They had been married for eighteen years at that point and had a total of nine children, although two children were indicated as deceased. The children enumerated included: Lula, sixteen; Arcus, fourteen; Modeson

(Matterson), twelve; Joseph, ten (my grandfather); Viola, eight; Mary F., six; and Mantley, one. Sadly in 1917, Frances died of paralysis, as indicated on her death certificate. Although this happened seven years after the census indicated her age was thirty-eight, on her death certificate, her age was reported as thirty-six.

By the 1920 census, John was a fifty-one-year-old widow living on Upper Enterprise Road in Coffee Springs, Geneva County. Living with him were three sons Arcus, twenty-three; Madison (Matterson), twenty-two; Mantley, eleven; two daughters, Dolly M., sixteen, and Mary Frances, 13; and Obe McNair, a boarder. In a rented dwelling on Kyles's farm lived his seventy-five-year-old mother, Dolly, and his brother John C., who was sixty. In another rented dwelling on Kyles's farm lived Marvin Fitzpatrick and his wife. In 1921, John married Sarah Baldwin. Sadly, in June 1925, John's mother, Dollie, died. Her age listed on her death certificate was ninety. The cause of death was listed as senility. Her age was reported as seventy-five on the 1920 census, which was inaccurate.

A notice of the register's sale appeared on February 15, 1924, in the first edition of the *Geneva County Reaper*.

The Union Mercantile Company was listed as the complainant against J.H. Kyles et al., the defendants, in the circuit court case. The notice indicated that "by virtue of a decree in the above-stated cause rendered by the circuit court, in equity to satisfy the decree, I will sell to the highest and best bidder for cash, at public sale, at the courthouse door of said county, between the hours of 11 a.m. and 4 p.m. on Monday, the 17th day of March 1924." The property for sale was described as the western half of the southeast quarter of the northwestern quarter (western half of the southeast quarter of northwest quarter) of section 34, township 3, and range 21 situated in Geneva County, Alabama. Documents to substantiate the court proceedings had not been obtained at the time of this writing. Although the land, in this case, represented about twenty acres of the Kyles homestead, several questions remain regarding the series of events that led to this property sale incident.

The 1930 census enumerated John (Henry), forty-eight, and his wife, Sarah, thirty-six, and recorded that they lived on Ezell Bridge Road in Center Geneva in a home that they owned. His occupation was listed as farmer working on his own account. In the household were the couple's four children: Corabelle (Carrie Belle), eight; Lucius, six; Roy, four; and Vela (Vedie M.), fourteen months. All of John's children from his first marriage were living elsewhere.

The oral history shared with the family says that John and other farmers experienced three years of low crop production caused by poor weather and other conditions. This occurred at the height of the Great Depression. When his crops did not produce the expected income from the sale of corn, wheat, cucumbers and other vegetables, he borrowed a small loan from the bank to buy fertilizer and other supplies to get his crops planted in the second and third years. At the end of the third year, he had a remaining debt said to be around forty dollars that he was unable to repay to the bank. As a result, his land was seized by the bank.

Between 1935 and 1940, John moved his family from what was formerly his homestead in Geneva. The 1940 census enumerated John, seventy-two, and Sarah, forty-six, and recorded that they lived in a rented home in Leverett, Coffee County, Alabama. John's occupation was listed as farm laborer, and it was recorded that he had worked for thirty-nine weeks in 1939. His reported income was $150. It was indicated that he had no other source of income. Living in the household were two daughters, Carrie Belle, seventeen, and Vedie M., eleven; two sons, Roy, fourteen, and Nathaniel, nine; and a niece, Minnie Phillips. A review of the census revealed no familiar names of any neighbors from the prior census records. At the time of this writing, there was no evidence that any of the homesteaders remained in the family that the original homestead, located at what is now known as 628 Old Elba Road, remained in the family.

John Henry Kyles and his two wives, Frances Eddins and Sarah Baldwin, created an extended family of hundreds of descendants in Alabama, Florida, New York, New Jersey, Ohio, Michigan and many other locations. My grandfather Joe Kyles was one of twelve children. He migrated north to Vassar, Michigan, in the mid-1940s with several other families from the Geneva and Coffee County communities in search of jobs in the manufacturing industry. This homesteading story is a powerful and bittersweet example of one man's effort to build a life for his family and the challenges associated with obtaining and then losing a homestead.

I now own the sepia-toned picture of John Henry Kyles and his wife, Francis Eddins Kyles, that once hung in Grandpa Joe's front room. It has a new meaning every time I see it, and it fills me with pride and admiration. Although I never met my great-grandparents, the ability to share this portion of their story makes me feel more connected to them. Their collective lives demonstrate the power of hard work, perseverance and neighbors who help each other to achieve a shared and communal goal.

The next step in this story is to explore tax and court records to determine the chain of ownership, including the current owners of John Kyles's former homestead. Another step will be to write the stories of the witnesses who appeared on John Kyles's homestead application. Some offspring of the witnesses' families eventually married Kyle's offspring. Their homestead stories also deserve to be told. It's my honor to contribute to the effort to memorialize the history of our ancestors who were homesteaders of the South.

CONTRIBUTOR: *Dr. Mary K. Clark considers herself a fact-teller rather than a storyteller. Her nonfiction stories are based on lived experiences and memories that have been collected in over thirty years of journal writing. Her story, "Armored by Hope: Shielded from Fear" appears in the Overcomers' Anthology, vol. 2, Overcoming Fear, by Claire Aldin Publications, which was released in May 2021.*

ARKANSAS BLACK HOMESTEADERS

Until the lion has his or her own storyteller,
the hunter will always have the best part of the story.
—Nigerian proverb

According to data from the Homestead National Historical Park Service, a total of 74,620 homesteaders were approved and received land patents in Arkansas. The total acreage of homesteaded land was 33,328,000, which represented 24 percent of the land in the state.

The Black homesteaders are represented in Bradley, Sevier and Dexter Counties in Arkansas These were families who toiled against a trying backdrop of hostile southern biases toward them, as many had remained in the same communities where they had once been enslaved. Facing a new life in a post–Civil War Arkansas, some had sought the services of the Freedmen's Bureau in securing work contracts with former slave owners.

What makes this untold Arkansas story unique is that though these homesteaders had earned meager funds as sharecroppers during those early years of freedom, some could amass the funds needed to acquire small pieces of personal property. In addition, their eyes were set on a higher goal—to become landowners. These individuals once held in bondage knew that their lives would be enhanced when they could work their land and keep their entire crop. The stories are wonderful reads into little-known Arkansas Black history—the story of Black families on the land who can tell their version of their "little house on the Arkansas prairie."

Sometimes, the Arkansas homesteads were carved out of timberland, such as the land in Sevier County, home of the old Norwoodville Timber Company, where many families were enslaved. With hard work, these families emerged not only as landowners but also as skilled laborers after they enrolled in Branch Normal College, which was opened in Arkansas for Black students. In another story, the reader will learn how one man almost lost an opportunity for land because he could not file the papers, as he was incarcerated. But through perseverance, he did obtain his land.

These stories from Arkansas are inspiring and will shed some light on little-known Black homesteaders of the South.

LEVI OR LEVY HAMPTON

By Jessica Trotter

Most records date Levi Hampton's birth around 1835 in Alabama, but we know little about his life before the Civil War. However, he was listed as a voter in 1867 in Bradley County, Arkansas, and was the head of a large household with his first wife, Dolly, in the 1870 census for Palestine Township. His children from this marriage included Mary H. (born around 1858), Edward (born around 1860), John (born around 1862), Will (born around 1864) and Lottie (born around 1869).

Per the homestead proof questionnaire, Hampton settled the land he would later claim as a homestead in section 22 with that family around January 1873. The actual Homestead Application no. 11408 was filed at the land office in Camden, Arkansas, on September 13, 1884, for 120 acres of timberland composed of white oak, pine and hickory trees.

From his first settlement in 1873 to his testimony as part of his proof packet, Hampton built an all-season log home, smokehouse, corncribs and stables, two cotton houses, plus an additional eighteen-by-eighteen-foot dwelling. He also cleared and fenced sixty acres of the land for cultivating corn and cotton. He had two mules, a horse and eight head of cattle. At the time of his proof, Hampton noted his family included "a wife and eight children" and that they had settled with him seventeen years prior. More accurately, during his homestead, the couple had at least one daughter, Anna, around 1874, before Dolly's death. Hampton married his second wife, Jane (also known as Virginia and Janey), Johnson in Bradley County on November 5, 1877, and they added a daughter, Lou, to the family in 1887.[54]

Levi Hampton formally proved for the land before the Bradley County Judge in Warren, Arkansas, on March 9, 1891, and signed by his mark. Close neighbors Sam Trotter and Ryal Trotter (neighboring brothers); an unrelated neighbor, Wilson Terry; and Will Newton (the Trotter's younger half-brother) were called as witnesses. Only Terry was on hand to stand for Hampton, and a note in the file asked the government to allow that. Homestead Certificate no. 5962 was officially signed on July 14, 1891. None of the others appear to have completed a homestead application.

The family appears to have prospered on the land, adding one more member of the family, Levi, and Jane's nephew Harrison Trotter (the son of Sam Trotter, mentioned previously, and Josephine Johnson) by the time of the 1910 census.[55] Trotter family lore credits Levi Hampton with helping raise and provide for Harrison, which appears to be supported by his bequest of seventeen acres to Harrison in his will from March 1916.[56] Some portion of the plot of land remains in the hands of the Trotter descendants to this day, and at one time, it housed Harrison Trotter and his fifteen children, including his eldest son, Levie, named in honor of Levi Hampton.

Levi Hampton willed seventeen acres to each of his remaining children (Ed, John, Will, Lottie Sims and Anna Nelson), plus Harrison Trotter, and eighteen acres passed to his widow, Jane. Levi passed some time before March 31, 1925, when his will was presented for execution.

CONTRIBUTOR: *Jessica Trotter is a librarian, genealogist and the great-granddaughter of Levi Hampton's nephew Harrison Trotter through his son, Levie.*

GIDEON MURPHY

By Lyle Gibson

Gideon H. Murphy settled on his land located in Sevier County, Arkansas, on January 18, 1879, and submitted Homestead Application no. 7236 on April 4, 1884, for 160 acres of land located on section 32, township 8s, range 29, 2 west.

He received Homestead Patent no. 3300 on January 1, 1885, for 160 acres, of which 15 to 16 acres were cleared for cultivation and included a two-room log house along with other outbuildings.

Gideon H. Murphy was born on July 27, 1846, in Sevier County, Arkansas, to Gideon "Gid" and Delilah Murphy, who had five other children, Lively "Comely" Murphy-Turrentine, born on February 4, 1839, in Sevier County, Arkansas, and died on May 22, 1916, in Sevier County, Arkansas; Ellen Murphy-Polk, born on May 12, 1842, in Sevier County, Arkansas, and died on February 11, 1918, in Howard County, Arkansas; Daniel W. Murphy, born in July 1849 in Sevier County, Arkansas, and died before 1910 in Sevier County, Arkansas; Arabella Murphy, born around 1854 in Sevier County, Arkansas, and died on June 4, 1937, in Sevier County, Arkansas; and Reuben Murphy (no additional information).[57]

Gideon H. Murphy was born on July 27, 1846, in Sevier County, Arkansas, to Gideon "Gid" and Delilah Murph. They had five other children all born in Sevier County. Lively "Comely" Murphy-Turrentine was born on February 4, 1839, and died on May 22, 1916. Ellen Murphy-Polk was born on May 12, 1842, and died on February 11, 1918, in Howard County, Arkansas. Daniel W. Murphy was born in July 1849 and died before 1910. Arabella Murphy was born around 1854 and died on June 4, 1937. There was no additional information about Reuben Murphy. Gideon and his parents and siblings were enslaved to Richard D. Murphy, the son of Cassandra Harpole and J.W. Murphy. Cassandra was the daughter of Captain John Harpole of Wilson County, Tennessee. Captain Harpole acquired land in southwest Arkansas Territory around 1817. He, his wife, Sarah, and their daughters moved from Wilson County, Tennessee, to Hempstead County, Arkansas Territory, around 1818. Their daughters were Mary Polly Harpole-Carr, Sarah Harpole-Props, Nancy Harpole-Hill and Margaret Harpole-Crabtree. Their grandchildren and the following enslaved individuals, Rueben, Lively, Sarah, Nancy, Winnie, Ben, Mary, Dolly, Minty, Gid (the father of Gideon H. Murphy), Hardy and Matilda, also moved to Hempstead County, Arkansas Territory around 1818.[58]

Gideon H. Murphy, along with his mother and siblings, are listed in the Freedmen's Bureau's records for the Paraclifta Office (Sevier County, Arkansas) from 1865 as having received rations. It is also documented that Murphy was on the Freedmen's Bank Records, dated June 26, 1873, his occupation listed as photographer.[59]

Per his testimony, Gideon stated that he had a wife and three children and that for two months, the family moved temporarily to "take care of crop" and that he had to attend to a "bad fence."

Per the 1880 Sevier County, Arkansas census, Gideon was enumerated with his wife, Allice, and their four-month-old daughter, Mereda. He was living next to his brother Dan Murphy, their mother, Delilah, and sister Arabella.[60]

The oral tradition of the Harpole family was passed down from Mariah "Big Sis" Harpole, the aunt of Gideon H. Murphy. Mariah was born around 1838 in Arkansas and died in 1911 in Howard County, Arkansas. Mariah was married to Reuben Harpole. Mariah helped raise many of her nieces and nephews and her two younger siblings, hence her nickname "Big Sis." Mariah's siblings were Gideon Harpole Murphy, born around 1816 in Tennessee; Hardy Harpole Murphy, born in 1817 in Tennessee and died in 1885 in Sevier County, Arkansas; Winnie Harpole, born around 1817 in Tennessee; Angeline Harpole-Booker, born around 1836 in Arkansas; Tilman Patterson Harpole, born on January 6, 1842, in Lafayette County, Arkansas, and died on April 11, 1916, in Kansas City, Missouri; and Catherine Kate Harpole-Burrell, born in March 1842 in Lafayette County, Arkansas, and died on March 10, 1927, in Lafayette County, Arkansas. DNA technology is bridging the gap of history and slavery, as descendants of Winnie Harpole, Angeline Harpole-Booker, Tilman P. Harpole and Kate Harpole-Burrell, share DNA matches helping reconstruct the family tree.[61]

Per the Homestead application and the Freedmen's Bank record, Gideon signed his name. The 1880 and 1900 censuses verify his literacy.

The witnesses were Frank W. Hall, James M. Hunsucker, Standford Hunsucker and Robert Watson. Mr. Watson, who stated that in the winter of 1879, Gideon had a "log house with two rooms and other outbuildings and about sixteen acres of land cleared and in cultivation." He cultivated crops over "five seasons."

CONTRIBUTOR: *Lyle Gibson is the 1st cousin five times removed of Gideon H. Murphy. Gibson's 4th great-grandmother Winnie Harpole was the aunt of Gideon H. Murphy. A genealogist with thirty-one years of experience and a historian with over twenty years of teaching experience developed an interest in history and genealogy.*

REUBEN MURPHY

By Lyle Gibson

Reuben Murphy settled on his land located in Sevier County, Arkansas, in 1878 and submitted Homestead Application no. 9150 on February

25, 1881, for the amount of six dollars for forty acres located on section 33, township 10s, range 29, northeast quarter of the northwest quarter. He was forty-two years old at the time he filed his application (although census records indicate he was around the age of thirty-six).

He received Homestead Patent Certificate no. 4452 on January 1, 1885, for forty acres, of which twenty acres were cleared for cultivation and included a dwelling house, corncrib, two stables, a blacksmith shop and a wall valued at $190.

Per the homestead application, Reuben signed with an X.

Per his testimony in February 1887, Reuben stated that he was the "head of a family," with a "wife and six children." He stated that he had claimed residence for nine years, and for nine seasons, he raised corn and cotton on twenty acres of cleared land. Additionally, Reuben stated that his taxes had been paid every year in Sevier County, Arkansas.

The witnesses were Walter Hopkins and Isom Carr. Hopkins stated that Reuben Murphy and his family settled on the land in 1878 and that Reuben built a "log and plank dwelling with three rooms," one sixteen by eighteen feet, another fifteen by sixteen feet and the third room fourteen by sixteen feet. He went on to state that the land was worth two dollars per acre. Hopkins had known Reuben Murphy for twenty years and also verified that the number of acres cleared and under cultivation was twenty. He confirmed that the crops raised were corn and cotton. Hopkins signed with an X. Mr. Carr, twenty-four, stated that he had known Reuben Murphy for seven years. His testimony aligned with the testimony of Walker Hopkins.

Reuben Murphy was born in July 1846 in Sevier County, Arkansas, to Gideon "Gid" and Delilah Murphy, who had five other children, Lively "Comely" Murphy-Turrentine, born on February 4, 1839, in Sevier County, Arkansas, and died on May 22, 1916, in Sevier County, Arkansas; Ellen Murphy-Polk, born on May 12, 1842, in Sevier County, Arkansas, and died on February 11, 1918, in Howard County, Arkansas; and Gideon Henry Murphy, born on July 27, 1846, in Sevier County, Arkansas, and died on January 18, 1930, in Howard County, Arkansas. Gideon also received a homestead certificate in 1885; Daniel W. Murphy was born in July 1849 in Sevier County, Arkansas, and died before 1910 in Sevier County, Arkansas; and Arabella Murphy was born around 1854 in Sevier County, Arkansas, and died on June 4, 1937, in Sevier County, Arkansas.[62]

Reuben and his parents and siblings were enslaved to Richard D. Murphy, the son of Cassandra Harpole and J.W. Murphy.[63]

Reuben Murphy, along with his mother and siblings, are listed on the Freedmen's Bureau records for the Paraclifta Office (Sevier County, Arkansas) in 1865 as having received rations.[64]

Per the 1880 Sevier County, Arkansas census, Reuben was enumerated with his wife, Nettie, and their children, Sarah, nine; Mary, seven; and Emy, one. Reuben and Nettie had additional children, Annie Murphy, born in 1881; Fred Murphy, born in 1883; Charles Murphy, born in 1885; Ben Hubert Murphy, born in 1887; and Allie Beatrice Murphy, born in 1890.[65]

There is no known information on Reuben Murphy after the 1910 census.[66]

The oral tradition of the Harpole family was passed down from Mariah "Big Sis" Harpole, the aunt of Gideon H. Murphy. Mariah was born around 1838 in Arkansas and died in 1911 in Howard County, Arkansas. Mariah was married to Reuben Harpole. Mariah helped raise many of her nieces and nephews and her two younger siblings, hence her nickname "Big Sis." Mariah's siblings were Gideon Harpole Murphy, born around 1816 in Tennessee; Hardy Harpole Murphy, born in 1817 in Tennessee and died in 1885 in Sevier County, Arkansas; Winnie Harpole, born around 1817 in Tennessee; Angeline Harpole-Booker, born around 1836 in Arkansas; Tilman Patterson Harpole, born on January 6, 1842, in Lafayette County, Arkansas, and died on April 11, 1916, in Kansas City, Missouri; and Catherine Kate Harpole-Burrell, born in March 1842 in Lafayette County, Arkansas, and died there on March 10, 1927.

CONTRIBUTOR: *Lyle Gibson is the first cousin five times removed of Gideon H. Murphy. Gibson's great-great-great-great-grandmother Winnie Harpole was the aunt of Gideon H. Murphy. He is a genealogist with thirty-one years of experience and a historian with over twenty years of teaching experience who developed an interest in history and genealogy.*

DON AND MINNIE-LEE McCORMICK

By Susan Lasley

He was born Singleton Don McCormick on February 10, 1872, in Robeson County, North Carolina. His parents, who had been born into slavery, were Willie and Adeline "Cinderella" Page McCormick. Don was the middle child, the fourth of the McCormicks' seven children listed in the 1880 U.S.

census for Thompson Township, North Carolina. She was born Minnie-Lee Wainwright on December 27, 1897, in Gibson County, Tennessee, as the first child of Amanda Cumbery, who was born into slavery in Tennessee. Her birth father's full name is lost to history, but when her mother married Sam Robinson, she changed her and her young daughter's surnames to match that of her husband.

Sometime during the 1880s, Don McCormick's parents moved the family from North Carolina to Arkansas. Don's niece Bessie McCormick Price gave an oral history passed down to her by her father (and Don's youngest brother), Chalmers McCormick. Chalmers told her that when he was a little boy, his father, Willie, was given a team of mules and a wagon and told to head west, following the river trails. Their parents were attracted by the work available in the timber industry, and recruiters were actively seeking formerly enslaved people from southeastern slave states to move to Arkansas.

In addition, they were attracted by the prospect of owning land and this public land was not available to them in eastern states like North Carolina. Don's granddaughter Bonnie McCormick McGlown had given an oral history stating that Don owned land in Jefferson County; a search of the records revealed a land patent granted in 1903.

Don McCormick married Minnie Lee Robinson on February 7, 1897. Minnie-Lee's family had also migrated to Arkansas from Tennessee. By the time Don had filed their final homestead proof, they had three children, Willie, Amanda and Nellie.

Don settled on his land in March 1894 and took residency a couple of months later in May. He filed his homestead affidavit on March 7, 1894, made formal application no. 19986 and paid a thirteen-dollar application fee.

Four of Don's neighbors, Henry J. McEachern, Milton Hill, John Harris and David Rose, had also traveled from North Carolina, South Carolina and Virginia to settle in Arkansas during westward migration. McEachern and Hill would later testify as witnesses on Don's final proof. One of the neighbors, David Rose, had already received his land patent in 1890.

Don and Minnie-Lee McCormick almost lost their chance to own the land they had cultivated and worked for years. By March 1902, after eight years of effort, Don missed an important deadline for his final affidavit for an important reason: he was locked up in jail.

In a separate affidavit Don filed on August 8, 1903, with the county clerk of Jefferson County, he stated that he could not make the final proof

Left: Don McCormick. *Right*: Minnie Lee McCormick. *Courtesy of Susan Lasley.*

in time because between March and May 1902, he was confined to the Jefferson County Jail, "charged with unlawfully cutting state land timber." He further stated that he was eventually acquitted of the charge and released from jail.

Don went on to file his final proof in late May 1902, but about a week later, the Land Office in Little Rock, Arkansas, indicated that his proof was not received in time. The official reasons they gave were that he "was in prison at the time" and under "duress." The Little Rock Land Office approved his application anyway, and it was subject to confirmation by the board. The land he staked for his claim was timberland. His witnesses said Don had cultivated three to seven acres over seven seasons. He built two "box houses" and a stable, with the total improvements valued between $100 and $150 in 1902. Don filed his proof of publication as required in the *Pine Bluff Graphic*, a weekly newspaper. The published advertisements appeared for six weeks, beginning in April 1902.

That approval from the board was confirmed on October 5, 1903. Don and Minnie-Lee received their land patent. It was granted on October 23, 1903, and then issued on October 26, 1903, for 120 acres of land in Jefferson County, Arkansas.

Don McCormick had been taught to read and write. Documents contained in his application file from the National Archives show his original signatures. The file also included a letter he wrote in his handwriting to J.E. Bush, the receiver at the Little Rock Land Office:

Dexter Ark. 03/29/1902

Mr. JE Bush, Sir,

Inclosed [sic] *Please find* [illegible] *fee and commission and I also send proof of publication from the editor of the* Graphic. *Please accept it and please let me hear from again if possible. Please oblige.*

Don McCormick
Dexter

The Little Rock Land Office obliged. Through hard work, a suspicious arrest, incarceration and a court trial, Don and Minnie-Lee McCormick got their 120 acres of land, the land patent confirmed in certificate no. 10455. Don McCormick died on February 4, 1925. Minnie-Lee remarried after he died, and on February 8, 1946, she died as Minnie-Lee Ware.

CONTRIBUTOR: *Susan Lasley is the great-granddaughter of Don and Minnie Lee McCormick and the granddaughter of Amanda McCormick Lasley, who was one of Don and Minnie Lee's three young children living on the land at the time the land patent was granted. She is a writer and historian who grew up in Arkansas and now lives in New York.*

IRVING BASS

By Angela Walton-Raji

Irving Bass was the oldest son of Louis Mitchell and Susan Bass from Sevier County, Arkansas. He was born in 1869 in the early years of freedom for his parents. His youth was spent in the small timberland community of Clear Creek in Sevier County. In those early years in the rural community of southwest Arkansas, formerly enslaved families had to work their way through the maze of a hostile South. Bass's mother, Susan, was from the line of an enslaved family who were held in bondage by the Houston family, who had migrated to Arkansas from Alabama. Bass's father, originally from Tennessee, was taken to Arkansas after the slave owner in Tennessee died some years earlier.

Opportunities were limited for the children of formerly enslaved people in the Deep South, especially if there were no schools provided by the Freedmen's Bureau. However, they had an interest in education, as well as becoming landowners. That interest in Bass came from his father, who made a lasting impression on his son. Although his father had been enslaved by Henry Pride in Sevier County, when freedom came, he chose a different name than that of Pride. He chose to be known as Louis Mitchell Bass, honoring his own family from Tennessee.

Irving Bass. *Courtesy of Angela Walton-Raji.*

In 1865, four years before Irving was born, Mitchell's name was placed on a labor contract through the Freedmen's Bureau with the former slaveholder.[67] It was stated on that record that he agreed to work for "board, clothing and medical attention." Interestingly, no monetary payment was part of that initial agreement. However, Mitchell was still able to work, grow crops and save a small amount of money, enough to have a small amount of personal property during those years. The federal census of Sevier Arkansas indicated that Lewis M. Bass had a small amount of property valued at $150 at the time.[68] Though not much in value, he had property in a time when the other formerly enslaved families in the same county and township did not have any.

In 1882, when Irving Bass was twelve years old, his father made a cash payment for forty acres of land, some of the public lands available in the area. His father, Mitchell, had become a proper landowner. This was not common in that county. Irving saw the advantage that his father had as a landowner, and this inspired him to do the same someday.

He also knew that his father could manage so much more if he were able to help him keep the books on the estate and manage their accounts without having to rely on others who could read. It was not long before Irving left home to get that education, and went away, to Pine Bluff Arkansas to go to school. A school had been established in Pine Bluff known as Branch Normal school. During the summer months, Bass was at home in

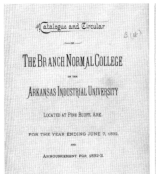

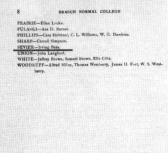

Irving Bass. *From the catalogue of Branch Normal College of the Arkansas Industrial University, located in Pine Bluff, Arkansas, for the year ending on June 9, 1893; the Daniel Murray Pamphlet Collection, Library of Congress.*

Sevier County, working the land with his father, Mitchell, but in the colder months, he was away at school for months at a time.[69]

Within a few short years, Irving would return and become the schoolteacher in the small country school that was later established for the Black children of Horatio, Arkansas. Some of his younger siblings would, in later years, speak about their first teacher being their older brother Irving Bass.

Before teaching, at the age of eighteen, Bass began working on his personal plan to become his own man. He established residence on a small plot of land in 1887. By 1890, he had a small log house with two rooms.[70] Meanwhile, during the early years, he continued to pursue an education, and shortly after selecting the land that he wished to live on, he balanced several years going back and forth between his country town and Pine Bluff, pursuing an education.

On his homestead application, when asked about whether he had resided on the land, his response was, "I was off the place for the purpose of going to school." He also noted that he had still worked "twelve to twenty acres for five seasons." To devote himself to two such endeavors at the same time— going to school and farming the land—was truly remarkable for any man, especially in later nineteenth-century rural Arkansas. Half the year, he was in school obtaining his education, and the other half of the year, he worked the land with his father.

Finally, at the mere age of twenty-six, he submitted his claim for a homestead. The land was located in the western half of the northwest quarter and the southeast quarter of the northwest quarter of section 7, township 10s, range 31, west. There were four witnesses to his claim. They were Louis Bass, Henry Dillahunty, John Martin and James Rice. Irving was quite close to two of the witnesses. One was his father, Louis Mitchell Bass, and another was a half-brother, John Martin. Dillahunty and Rice were close associates of the family.

Irving and his father worked together on all the family-owned lands, and an interview with one of his sisters in 1878, it was revealed that other families in the area also lived on Bass land, as they were allowed to rent small parcels of land from them and would pay the Bass landowners—both father and son—to use the land. [71]

Like his father, Irving Bass became his own man, owning 120 acres, becoming a landlord and renting portions of his land to other families in the area and becoming an educated man and a teacher in the local school. And like other literate men, when he claimed his homestead, he proudly signed his name.[72]

Clearly, Bass's story is a success story of how this young man accomplished his dreams in a hostile southern community and became an independent landowner and leader in the community. Irving would later marry Eliza Martin, who was part of a large family of Martins in the area, and together, they raised their children on the family land in Horatio, where they lived well into the 1940s.

The children of Irving Bass would later migrate westward to Arizona and California, and after he retired from teaching, he joined the family out west, where he and Eliza spent their remaining years. The story of Irving Bass is that of a young boy with vision who accomplished his goals against all odds. The descendants of his family went forward from the nurturing that began on Arkansas soil on a small parcel of land of the homesteader Irving Bass.

CONTRIBUTOR: *Angela Walton-Raji has researched her family from western Arkansas and eastern Oklahoma for over thirty years. On the Arkansas side, her paternal grandmother came from Sevier County, Arkansas. Her grandfather Louis Mitchell Bass became a landowner in 1882, making a cash payment for forty acres.*

3

FLORIDA BLACK HOMESTEADERS

In all of us there is a hunger, marrow-deep,
to know our heritage—to know who we are and where we have come from.
—Alex Haley

According to data from the Homestead National Historical Park Service, a total of 28,096 homesteaders were proved up in Florida. The total acreage of homesteaded land was 3,326,712, which is 10 percent of the land in the state.

This chapter brought together four genealogists who submitted stories about six individuals that obtained homestead land in late nineteenth-century Florida. In this chapter, Margo Lee Williams, Falan Goff and Deborah Mitchell share their Florida homesteader stories and unique family recollections. Orice Jenkins also discovered that legendary singer Whitney Houston was a descendant of a Black homesteader from Florida.

Margo Lee Williams, an award-winning author and genealogist/family historian, submitted three stories celebrating her paternal family heritage in Suwannee County: a great grandfather, a great-great-step-grandfather and a great-granduncle's father-in-law. Margo was aware from an early age that her family had owned property in Live Oak, Suwannee County. However, it was only after beginning her research to locate information in the relevant deeds that she learned her ancestors had applied for and been awarded homestead patents. After discussions with other homesteader descendants, she searched for and discovered the names of an additional forty-four

Suwannee County Black homesteaders who are listed in the appendix with their corresponding dates of proof.

Falan Goff, a genealogist/family historian, contributed the story of her relative Simon Bell. Falan was not aware of any farmers or landowners from that time in her family. Over her extensive career in agriculture and genealogy, Goff was adamant that she had no family ties to the agricultural community or landowners until she found Simon Bell. The most rewarding part about finding Simon was that she was able to give her ninety-two-year-old grandmother details of her family history. Simon became the motivation that led Goff to discover more Black Floridian homesteaders. Deborah Mitchell is an avid family history buff and has been researching the genealogy of her family for over 30 years. She discovered the homestead patent for her ancestor but only recently obtained a copy of his land entry case files.

ALEXANDER GAINER

By Margo Lee Williams, MA

William Gainer Williams, grandfather. *Courtesy of Margo Lee Williams.*

Alexander "Alex" Gainor/Gainer was my paternal, great-great-stepgrandfather. He was married to my grandfather's (William Gainer Williams) mother's (Ellen Wilkinson Williams) mother, Frances (Smiley) Gainer.[73] I do not know very much about his life before emancipation. According to my aunt Lute Williams Mann, he fought in the Civil War and lost a leg. However, I found no evidence that he served in any Union forces and can only conclude he had been forced to work for the Confederate army, though in what capacity, I do not know. The only information I can verify about his early life comes from the census, where his home state is listed as South Carolina. All documentation about his life that I have been able to locate pertains to his life in Suwannee County, Florida.

The earliest record available for "Aleck Gainer" was a record of his voter registration from August 20, 1867, in Live Oak. Interestingly, it has a line crossed through it. The notations indicate he was living in the county for

Alex Gainer's homestead, initial affidavit. *Homestead Land Entry Papers, application no. 5609, NARA.*

four months. The column that indicates whether he voted wasn't checked. Otherwise, there is nothing noted.[74]

In September 1868, the Pensacola and Georgia Railroad sold land in Live Oak to Alex and his stepson-in-law, George Manker.[75] In 1870, Alexander and my great-great-grandmother Frances were listed in the census with their son, Edward.[76] However, Alex and Frances were not formally married until 1874, when they were married by Robert Allen, a minister at the Baptist Church now called the African Baptist Church.[77] The 1870s would see Frances purchase property (in 1871 and 1874), but Alex would not purchase property again until he completed his homestead claim in 1877.[78]

On May 11, 1872, Alex filed his application, no. 5609, for a homestead claim of 39.89 acres.[79] On the same date, he swore an affidavit stating that he had filed the claim but "by reason of distance" could not personally

State of Florida
Suwannee County }

On this First day of June A.D. 1877.
personally come Robert Allen and
Caleb Simpkins who being duly sworn
depose and say that they have known
Alexander ~~Gaines~~ since June 14th 1872
and that the said Alexander Garner has occupied and cultivated and improved the
N E¼ of S E¼ of Section 26 Township 2,
South of Range 13 East as a homestead
from the date above continuously from
the date above to the present time, And
that this affidavit is sworn to enable him
to complete his title to the said homestead,
and that they are unable to attend the
General Land Office to give evidence in
his behalf on account of distance and
want of means to pay their expenses.

Sworn & Subscribed to
before me June 1st 1877

M. M. Blackburn
Justice of the Peace

and he has built a house there on, & cultivated about 10 acres.
and made other valuable improvements

Robert X Allen
his mark

Caleb X Simpkins
his mark

State of Florida }
Suwannee County }

I do hereby certify that the above witnesses
are credible and responsible as such.
Given under my hand and official Seal on
this June 1st, 1877. -   M. M. Blackburn
                                      Justice of the Peace.

Final Affidavit Required of Homestead Claimants.

Act of May 20, 1862.

I, *Alexander Gainor* , having made a Homestead entry of the *N E ¼ of S E ¼* section No. *26.* in township No. *2 S* , of range No. *13 E.* subject to entry at *Tallahassee* . *now Gainesville* under the first section of the Homestead Act of *May 20, 1862* , do now apply to perfect my claim thereto by virtue of the first proviso to the second section of said act; and for that purpose do solemnly *swear* that *I am* a citizen of the United States; that I have made actual settlement upon and have cultivated said land, having resided thereon since the *14* day of *June* , 18 *72* to the present time; that no part of said land has been alienated, but that I am the sole bona fide owner as an actual settler; and that I will bear true allegiance to the Government of the United States. *and that I have not heretofore perfected or abandoned an entry under this act.*

his
Alexander X Gainor
mark

I, *J. A. Lee Register* , of the Land Office at *Gainesville* , do hereby certify that the above affidavit was taken and subscribed before me this *14* day of *June* , 187 *7* .

J A Lee Register

HOMESTEAD.

Land Office at *Gainesville Fla June 14th , 1877*

FINAL CERTIFICATE, No. *12__* } { APPLICATION, No. *5609*

It is hereby certified That, pursuant to the provisions of Section No. 2291, Revised Statutes of the United States, *Alexander Gainor* , has made payment in full for *North East ¼ of South East ¼*

of Section No. *Twenty-six (26)* , in Township No. *Two (2) South* of Range No. *Thirteen (13) East*, containing *Thirty-Nine + 89/100* acres.

NOW, THEREFORE, BE IT KNOWN, That on presentation of this Certificate to the COMMISSIONER OF THE GENERAL LAND OFFICE, the said *Alexander Gainor* shall be entitled to a Patent for the Tract of Land above described.

J A Lee Register.

Opposite: The witness testimony of Caleb Simpkins and Robert Allen. *Homestead Land Entry Papers, application no. 5609, NARA.*

Top: Alex Gainer's final affidavit. *Homestead Land Entry Papers, application no. 5609, NARA.*

Bottom: Alex Gainer's final certificate. *Homestead Land Entry Papers, application no. 1236, NARA.*

appear at the land office in Tallahassee.[80] On June 14 ,1872, a receiver's receipt for seven dollars paid to the receiver's office in Tallahassee was created.[81]

On June 1, 1877, Alex's witnesses, Caleb Simpkins and Robert Allen (the Baptist minister who married him), gave their testimony on behalf of his claim.[82] They testified that since June 14, 1872, Alex had occupied, cultivated and improved the northeast quarter of the southeast quarter of section 26, township 2, south of range 13, east, as a homestead. They also testified that "this affidavit was made to enable him to complete his title to the said homestead."

Their testimony goes on to say that they were unable to go to the general land office to give their testimony "on account of distance and want of means to pay the expenses." Thus, they gave their testimony before the justice of the peace "M.M. Blackburn" in Suwannee County; both signed with an X. An additional sentence was added after their signatures, saying, "And he has built a house thereon and cultivated about ten acres and made other valuable improvements."[83]

On June 14, 1877, Alex made his final affidavit in support of his claim. He stated that he had settled and cultivated his claim land since June 14, 1872, that he hadn't "alienated" the land and that he was the sole

owner and actual settler. He swore that he bore allegiance to the United States "and that I have not heretofore perfected or abandoned an entry und this act."[84] After paying an additional and final two dollars to the receiver in the Gainesville office, he received his final certificate, no. 1236.[85] Notations in the file indicate, however, that final approval was not given until May 11, 1878, and the patent was not recorded until June 24, 1878, in Land Record Book, vol. 3, page 26.[86]

Alex did not record the deed with the Suwannee County registrar right away. In June 1886, the homestead claim was filed, finally in Book J, page 288. However, in the very next entry, "Alexandre Gainer" sold to Justice of

Ellen Williams, Alex Gainer's stepdaughter and this author's great-grandmother. *Courtesy of Margo Lee Williams.*

the Peace M.M. Blackburn the same property for $500.[87] Alex appeared for the last time in the deed records in January 1887, when he and Frances sold another property to Frances's daughter Carry "Corra" Manker, the widow of George Manker.[88]

It is assumed Alex died sometime between 1887 and 1896, when his "widow," Frances, sold property to James Moore and C.J. Manker, her grandson.[89] It is believed Frances died between 1896 and 1900. She does not appear in the 1900 census. In 1901 and 1911, her daughters, Carry Manker and Ellen Williams (my great-grandmother), sold the property that was bought in 1868 by George Manker and Alex to Jesse Manker, Carry's grandson, and a Mamie Edwards.[90] With that, the last of the properties acquired by Alex and Frances during their marriage were passed to a new generation. Alex and Frances were buried in the inaccessible Old City Cemetery section of Eastside Memorial Cemetery in Live Oak, where most of their family members were buried.

SIMON BELL

By Falan Goff

Simon Bell was my maternal great-great-great uncle. His sister, Milly Bell, was my great-great-great-grandmother.[91] Simon "Sim" Bell was born in March 1842 in Florida.[92] On July 5, 1866, at twenty-four years old, he was married to Eliza "Liza" Bell.[93]

When Sim was about thirty years old, he applied for a homestead.[94] The land was located in Chattahoochee, Gadsden County, Florida.[95] He filed Homestead Application no. 5620 on June 26, 1872, at the county clerk's office in Tallahassee, Florida, for 39.94 acres.[96] He then filed his claim at the land office in Gainesville, Alachua County, Florida.[97] He paid seven dollars for the application filing fee.[98] He was granted a total of 39.94 acres in Chattahoochee. Currently, his land is surrounded by a street named Bell Street. His certificate lists the area as Section 10, Town 3N, Range 6W.

Sim was a witness on his own behalf in support of his homestead application, no. 1588, on December 16, 1878.[99] At the time of his application, Sim was the head of his family and had a total of four children living with him. Upon further research, he and his wife, Eliza, had a total of nine children.[100]

Left: Street marker "Bell." *Courtesy of Falan Goff.*

Opposite: Maud Humphries, this author's grandmother. *Courtesy of Falan Goff.*

Sim made a very revealing statement in his interview. He expressed that he was a "native-born citizen of the United States by the Emancipation Proclamation of President Lincoln." This statement leads one to believe he was born in the United States but was previously enslaved. Sim alluded that he was freed from slavery after the Emancipation Proclamation. He used his homestead application as an opportunity to acknowledge that he was freed from slavery.

As noted earlier, Sim and his family settled on the land on June 26, 1872, and established residence around September or October 1, 1872. He made improvements to his land that included nine houses and about thirty acres of cultivated land. The first house Sim built was constructed in October 1872, and its improvements were valued around seventy-five dollars. On about thirty of his acres, Sim cultivated corn, cotton, sugarcane, potatoes, ground peas and rice. He specifically stated that he moved his family with him to the homestead and that they had resided there up to the time of the interview in December 1878.

In 1880, Sim lived on the land with Eliza and their children, along with his aunt Matilda Baker. Sim's homestead was finally issued on August 25, 1882.

In 1885, Sim Bell, Eliza and their children, along with his aunt Matilda Baker, remained on the homestead. The couple had a total of nine children. His children's names were Elville Bell, Eliza Bell, Meshader Bell, Josephine Bell Goldin, David Bell, Carry Bell and Ruth Bell Jones.

In 1885, Sim lived in Chattahoochee with thirty of his known family members as neighbors. This number mostly included his nieces and nephews. His sisters and brothers were listed in the census as Arthur Bell, Milly Bell-Smith and William Bell. Of Milly's six children, Lucinda (Eliza) Scott is my great-great-grandmother.

Sim continued living on his homestead land in 1900. The census states he was fifty-eight years old and a farmer who owned his home and farm. Twelve people lived with him at the time. Milly's daughter Lucinda Scott was twenty-four and was a family member living on Sim's homestead with her children, Maud L. Scott and Olivia Scott. Maud Lee and Olivia were Sim's grandnieces. Olivia Scott-Woods was my great-grandmother. Olivia's daughter Maud Woods-Humphries, my grandmother, is living today and is ninety-one years old.

Maud was made aware of her family through Sim's homesteading discovery. Maud always knew her family was from Gadsden County. She grew up knowing only a small number of relatives. She never knew how many relatives she truly had until now. When told the story of Simon, Maud stated that she "wished her mother was alive to know this."

It has been 149 years since Sim first settled on his land. When Maud was told that Simon was a farmer, she remembered that her family always kept the tradition of getting fresh vegetables and agricultural products from Chattahoochee. She recalled it being the best-tasting produce in the area. Maud was informed that Sim's land was less than a mile away from the Apalachicola River. She recalled that the only way they could travel to her hometown of Apalachicola from the Chattahoochee was along the river.[101] The Apalachicola River was a major mover of commerce during that time.

The homestead is no longer in the Bell family, but they made a trip to retrieve the soil. Maud Olivia Woods Humphries, ninety-one, is pictured holding a jar of red soil clay from her great-great-uncle Simon "Sim" Bell's homestead in Chattahoochee, Gadsden County, Florida. The jar is also sealed with a bell to represent her Bell ancestor.

RANDEL FARNELL

By Margo Lee Williams, MA

Randel Farnell was my paternal great-grandfather.[102] His daughter Lela was my father's mother. Randel was born in Hawkinsville, Pulaski County, Georgia, on March 15, 1840.[103] He was born to an enslaved mother, Maria Farnell, and a white father, James Farnell. James was the son of Elisha Farnell, who was born in Onslow County, North Carolina, moved to Laurens County, Georgia, and eventually settled in Pulaski County, Georgia, where he served as a state representative and senator.[104]

Elisha was also a substantial landowner, enslaving twenty-six people, including "Mareah, a girl," according to the estate inventory at the time of his death.[105] Maria was "distributed" to James.[106] Around 1850, James and his family moved to Florida, as did other Farnell family members.[107] James enlisted in the Confederate army in 1862. He was injured at Sharpsburg and died in a Confederate army hospital in Winchester, Virginia, on October 16, 1862.[108]

The end of the war found Randel, his wife, Sallie Jacobs, and their children listed in the 1870 census in Columbia County.[109] In 1876, after his mother, Maria, died, Randel moved from Columbia County, Florida,

Left: Randel Farnell, great-grandfather. *Right*: Lela Virginia Farnell Williams, grandmother. *Courtesy of Margo Lee Williams.*

to neighboring Suwannee County, where his wife's family, William and Charlotte Jacobs, and their other children lived.[110] A year later, on September 13, 1877, he filed Homestead Application no. 5637, at the county clerk's office in Live Oak. Randel applied for 39.78 acres. He then filed his claim at the land office in Gainesville, Alachua County, Florida. Although the land itself was free, he had to pay seven dollars for the application filing fee.[111]

Seven years later, on August 18, 1884, Randel appeared at the land office in Gainesville, again. At that time, he gave notice of his intent to present final proof to establish his claim to the land as defined in his application. He stated that he expected to prove his residence on and the cultivation of the land before the Honorable M.M. Blackburn in Live Oak, Suwannee County, on October 4, 1884. He stated that two of the four people named, Elijah Carruthers, Henry McGhee, Edward Perry and Puck Ferguson,

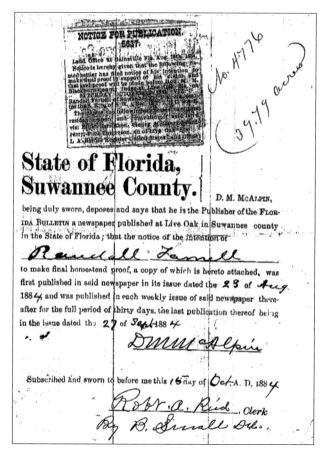

A public notice in *Florida Bulletin.* *Homestead Land Entry Papers, application no. 5647, NARA.*

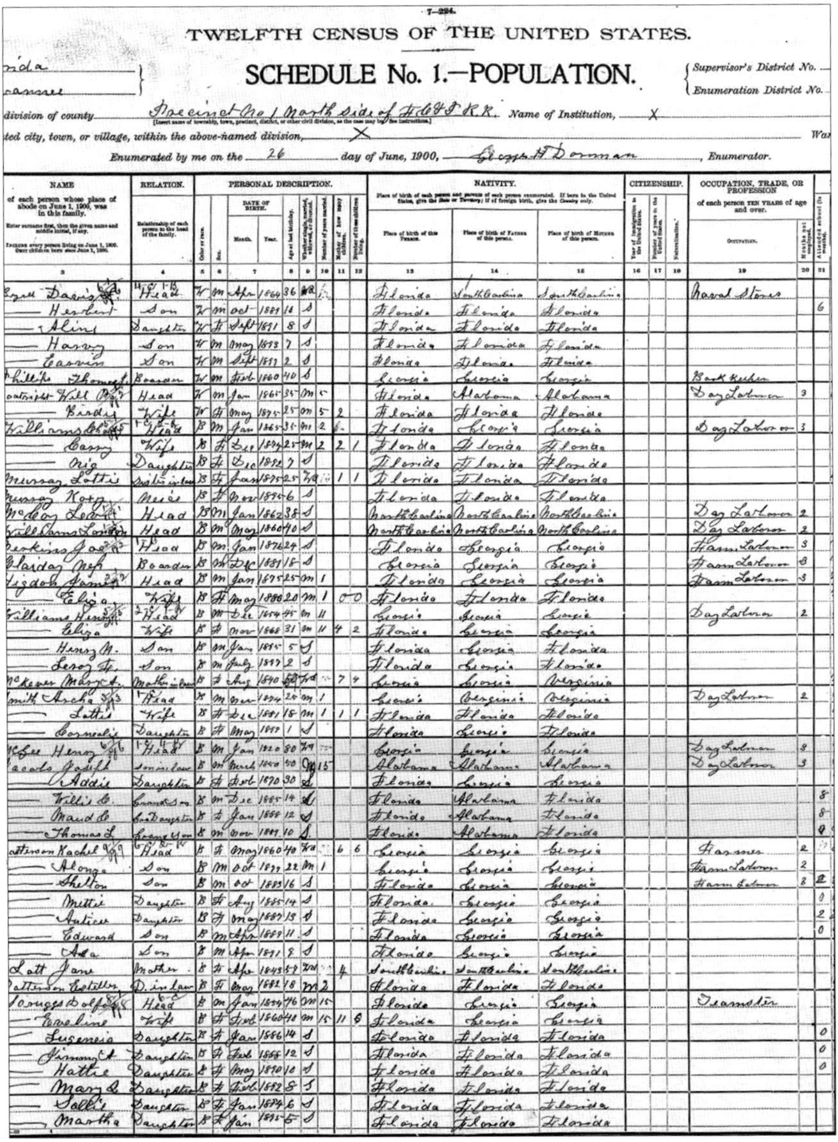

7—224.

TWELFTH CENSUS OF THE UNITED STATES.

SCHEDULE No. 1.—POPULATION.

[Flo]rida } Supervisor's District No.
[Suw]annee } Enumeration District No.

[Township or other] division of county: Precinct No. 1 North side of F.C.&P. R.R. Name of Institution, X

[Name of incorpora]ted city, town, or village, within the above-named division, X Ward

Enumerated by me on the 26 day of June, 1900, George H. Dorman, Enumerator.

Name	Relation	Color	Sex	Month	Year	Age	Marital	Yrs married	Children born	Living	Birthplace	Father's birthplace	Mother's birthplace	Occupation	Months not employed	School
[Ezell?] Davis	Head	W	M	Apr	1864	36	M				Florida	South Carolina	South Carolina	Naval Stores		
—— Herbert	Son	W	M	Oct	1881	18	S				Florida	Florida	Florida			6
—— Aline	Daughter	W	F	Sept	1891	8	S				Florida	Florida	Florida			
—— Harvey	Son	W	M	May	1893	7	S				Florida	Florida	Florida			
—— Carvin	Son	W	M	Sept	1897	2	S				Florida	Florida	Florida			
Phillips Thomas	Boarder	W	M	Feb	1860	40	S				Georgia	Georgia	Georgia	Book Keeper		
[Cartright?] Will	Head	W	M	Jan	1865	35	M	5			Florida	Alabama	Alabama	Day Laborer	3	
—— Birdie	Wife	W	F	May	1875	25	M	5	2		Florida	Florida	Florida			
Williams Charles	Head	B	M	Jan	1865	35	M	2			Florida	Georgia	Georgia	Day Laborer	3	
—— Carry	Wife	B	F	Dec	1874	25	M	2	2	1	Florida	Florida	Florida			
—— Nig	Daughter	B	F	Dec	1892	7	S				Florida	Florida	Florida			
Murray Lottie	Sister-in-law	B	F	Jan	1875	25	Wd		1	1	Florida	Florida	Florida			
Murray [illegible]	Neice	B	F	Nov	1895	6	S				Florida	Florida	Florida			
McCoy Leon	Head	B	M	Jan	1862	38	S				North Carolina	North Carolina	North Carolina	Day Laborer	2	
Williams London	Head	B	M	May	1860	40	S				North Carolina	North Carolina	North Carolina	Day Laborer	2	
Perkins Joe	Head	B	M	Jan	1876	24	S				Florida	Georgia	Georgia	Farm Laborer	3	
[illegible] Neh	Boarder	B	M	Dec	1881	18	S				Georgia	Georgia	Georgia	Farm Laborer	3	
[illegible] James	Head	B	M	Jan	1875	25	M	1			Florida	Georgia	Georgia	Farm Laborer	3	
—— Eliza	Wife	B	F	May	1880	20	M	1	0	0	Florida	Florida	Florida			
Williams Henry	Head	B	M	Dec	1854	45	M	11			Georgia	Georgia	Georgia	Day Laborer	2	
—— Eliza	Wife	B	F	Nov	1868	31	M	11	4	2	Florida	Georgia	Georgia			
—— Henry M.	Son	B	M	Jan	1895	5	S				Florida	Georgia	Florida			
—— Leroy F.	Son	B	M	July	1897	2	S				Florida	Georgia	Florida			
McKeever Mary A.	Mother-in-law	B	F	Aug	1840	59	Wd		7	4	Georgia	Georgia	Virginia			
Smith Archie	Head	B	M	Nov	1874	25	M	1			Georgia	Virginia	Virginia	Day Laborer	2	
—— Lottie	Wife	B	F	Dec	1881	18	M	1	1	1	Florida	Florida	Florida			
—— Cornelia	Daughter	B	F	May	1897	1	S				Florida	Georgia	Florida			
McGee Henry	Head	B	M	Jan	1820	80	Wd				Georgia	Georgia	Georgia	Day Laborer	3	
Jacobs Joseph	Son-in-law	B	M	March	1860	40	M	15			Alabama	Alabama	Alabama	Day Laborer	3	
—— Addie	Daughter	B	F	Feb	1870	30	M				Florida	Georgia	Georgia			
—— Willie E.	Grandson	B	M	Dec	1885	14	S				Florida	Alabama	Florida			8
—— Maud E.	Granddaughter	B	F	Jan	1888	12	S				Florida	Alabama	Florida			8
—— Thomas L.	Grandson	B	M	Nov	1889	10	S				Florida	Alabama	Florida			4
Patterson Rachel	Head	B	F	May	1860	40	Wd		6	6	Georgia	Georgia	Georgia	Farmer	2	
—— Alonzo	Son	B	M	Oct	1877	22	M	1			Georgia	Georgia	Georgia	Farm Laborer	2	
—— Shelton	Son	B	M	Oct	1883	16	S				Florida	Georgia	Georgia	Farm Laborer	2	2
—— Mittie	Daughter	B	F	Aug	1885	14	S				Florida	Georgia	Georgia			0
—— Antice	Daughter	B	F	May	1887	13	S				Florida	Georgia	Georgia			2
—— Edward	Son	B	M	Apr	1888	11	S				Florida	Georgia	Georgia			0
—— Ada	Son	B	M	Apr	1891	9	S				Florida	Georgia	Georgia			
Latt Jane	Mother	B	F	Apr	1845	55	Wd		4		South Carolina	South Carolina	South Carolina			
Patterson Estella	D. in law	B	F	May	1882	18	M	2			Florida	Florida	Florida			
[illegible] Dolph	Head	B	M	Jan	1854	46	M	15			Florida	Georgia	Georgia	Teamster		
—— Emeline	Wife	B	F	Feb	1860	40	M	15	11	8	Florida	Georgia	Georgia			
—— Eugenia	Daughter	B	F	Jan	1886	14	S				Florida	Florida	Florida			0
—— Jimmy A.	Daughter	B	F	Feb	1888	12	S				Florida	Florida	Florida			0
—— Hattie	Daughter	B	F	May	1890	10	S				Florida	Florida	Florida			0
—— Mary L.	Daughter	B	F	Feb	1892	8	S				Florida	Florida	Florida			
—— Sallie	Daughter	B	F	Jan	1894	6	S				Florida	Florida	Florida			
—— Martha	Daughter	B	F	Jan	1895	5	S				Florida	Florida	Florida			

would provide witness testimony. In addition, it was recorded that public notice of the homestead application would appear in the *Florida Bulletin*, published in Live Oak. That notice appeared for thirty days, beginning on August 23 and running until September 27, 1884. There was also a posting attested to by L.A. Barnes, a land office register, who certified that a printed copy of the notice was posted in his office for thirty days, beginning on August 18, 1884.[112]

[4—369.]

HOMESTEAD PROOF.—TESTIMONY OF WITNESS.

Henry McGhee .... being called as witness in support of the Homestead entry
of *Randall Farnell* .... for *the South East quarter of the South*
west quarter of Sec 12 T 2 R 13 S & E ...., testifies as follows:

Ques. 1.—What is your occupation and where is your residence?

Ans. *Farmer Suwannee County Florida*

Ques. 2.—Have you been well acquainted with *Randall Farnell* , the claimant, in

this case ever since he made his homestead entry No. *5637*

Ans. *Yes*

Ques. 3.—Was claimant qualified to make said entry? (State whether the settler was a citizen of the United States,

over the age of twenty-one years, or the head of a family, and whether he ever made a former homestead entry.)

Ans. *Yes. Citizen of the United States over the
age of 21 years & the head of a family, never made
any former homestead entry*

Ques. 4.—When did claimant settle upon the homestead and at what date did he establish actual residence thereon?

(Describe the dwelling and other improvements, giving total value thereof.)

Ans. *About 12 September 1877 Log Dwelling Splendid
Smoke house Crib Stables. 35 acres fenced & cultivated
value $200*

Ques. 5.—Have claimant and family resided continuously on the homestead since first establishing residence thereon?

(If settler is unmarried, state the fact.)

Ans. *Yes*

Ques. 6.—For what period or periods has the settler been absent from the land since making settlement, and for

what purpose; and if temporarily absent, did claimant's family reside upon and cultivate the land during such absence?

Ans. *Never absent except to labor at other places daily
at times. Family resided on Same & they themself Cultivated*

Ques. 7.—How much of the homestead has the settler cultivated and for how many seasons did he raise crops thereon?

Ans. *35 acres 7 Seasons*

Ques. 8.—Are there any indications of coal, salines, or minerals of any kinds on the homestead? (If so, describe

what they are, and state whether the land is more valuable for agricultural than for mineral purposes.)

Ans. *No*

Ques. 9.—Has the claimant mortgaged, sold, or contracted to sell, any portion of said homestead?

no

Opposite:
The Henry
McGhee
Household
in 1900, with
Joe Jacobs
and Henry's
daughter,
Addie McGhee
Jacobs. *Courtesy
of Margo Lee
Williams.*

Left: Henry
McGhee's
testimony.
*Homestead Land
Entry Papers,
application no.
5647, NARA.*

One month before the October 4 deadline, on September 4, Randel appeared before Suwannee County judge Blackburn and stated that he settled the land on September 12, 1877. The final testimonies of witnesses and Randel Farnell himself were given on October 4, 1884. Two men gave witness testimony. One, Henry McGhee, had been named in the initial application, while the other, William Evans, was not.[113] Henry McGhee's family and Randel's family would have long-lasting personal ties, as Henry's daughter Addie eventually married Randel's brother-in-law Joseph Jacobs.[114]

William Evans testified that Randel Farnell was a citizen of the United States over the age of twenty-one and the head of a family who had never made a claim for homestead property before. He went on to say that Randel had settled the homestead in 1877. He stated there was a "nice log house

Final Homestead Proof required under Section 2291 of the Revised Statutes of the United States.

WE, *Randall Farnall W F Bynum Jr*, do solemnly *Swear* that we have known *Henry McGehee* for *Seven* years last past; that he is *the head of a family* consisting of *himself & his wife* and *four* *children & he is* a citizen of the United States; that he is an inhabitant of the *North East Quarter of South West quarter* of Section No. *Twelve* in Township No. *Seven South* of Range No. *Thirteen Ea*, and that no other person resided upon the said land entitled to the right of Homestead or Pre-emption.

That the said *Henry McGehee* entered upon and made settlement on said land on the *first* day of *January*, 18 *70* and has built a house thereon *a good comfortable Log House with other improvements*

and has lived in the said house and made it his exclusive home from the *first* day of *January*, 18 *70*, to the present time, and that he has, since said settlement, plowed, fenced, and cultivated about *fifteen* acres of said land, and has made the following improvements thereon, to wit: *A good Log Dwelling House — Corn Crib — Smoke House — Good Garden and other improvements and with witness cannot appear at the land fifty miles failure*

Randall X Farnall
W F Bynum Jr

I, *William Forsyth Bynum*, do hereby certify that the above affidavit was taken and subscribed before me this *5th* day of *May*, 18 *77*, *and that the parties are perfectly responsible —*

Wm Forsyth Bynum Dept Clerk
Circuit Court Suwannee County Fla.

I *We* CERTIFY that *Randall Farnall and W F Bynum Jr*, whose names are subscribed to the foregoing affidavit, are persons of respectability.

J A SeC, Register.

, Receiver.

(dwelling) crib, smokehouse and stable, about thirty-five acres in cultivation, value $200." He stated that Randel and his family had resided on the homestead continuously since their first settlement. He said that they had not been absent from the property, except to "labor" at other places daily, but the family had "self-cultivated" the property. He further attested that there was no oil or other minerals and that the land was more valuable as agricultural land than for its mineral potential. He also affirmed that the property had not been mortgaged. Finally, he agreed he had no personal

HOMESTEAD.

Land Office at *Gainesville Fla*

Oct 29, 1884

FINAL CERTIFICATE,
No. 4776

APPLICATION.
No. 5637

It is hereby certified, That, pursuant to the provisions of Section No. 2291, Revised Statutes of the United States, *Randall Farnell* has made payment in full for *The South East quarter of South West quarter*

of Section No. *12* in Township No. *2 South*, of Range No. *13 East* of the *Tallahassee* Principal Meridian, containing *39 79/100* acres.

Now, therefore, be it known, That on presentation of this Certificate to the COMMISSIONER OF THE GENERAL LAND OFFICE, the said *Randall Farnell*

shall be entitled to a Patent for the Tract of Land above described.

L A Barnes

Register.

Area by plat 39.89

Opposite: Randel Farnell's testimony. *Homestead Land Entry Papers, application no. 5647, NARA.*

Left: The final certificate of Randel Farnell. *Homestead Land Entry Papers, application no. 4776, NARA.*

interest in the property. Henry McGhee's responses were similar. However, he called the log dwelling "splendid."

Randel was also required to testify. He reiterated all the things that Evans and McGhee stated. In addition, he was asked about his family. He responded that in addition to himself, there was his wife, Sallie (Jacobs) Farnell, a dressmaker, and six children. The word "four" had been crossed out; this was because he had four biological children (Maryland, William, Jackson and Lela) with his wife, and she had two additional children of her own (Anna and Richard).[115] Randel also noted that about thirty-five acres had been cultivated, on which he had raised crops for seven seasons.[116]

The final certificate, no. 4776, was issued on October 29, 1884, for 39.79 acres (one acre more than identified in the original application). The family continued to live on the property until around 1910, when they moved into the city of Live Oak, on Anderson Street, where Randel had a hauling business ("drayman").[117]

In 1906, Sallie died of Tuberculosis.[118] On December 26, 1907, Randel married a much younger woman, Priscilla Vickers.[119] On October 27, 1928, Randel died.[120] Amusingly, his death certificate stated he was one year older than his firstborn child, William. His widow, Priscilla, continued to live in the home on Anderson Street until she died in 1967.[121] The homestead property remained in the family until after her death, when my father and his siblings, the heirs, knowing they would never return to Florida to live, decided to sell the property.[122]

HENRY McGEHEE

By Margo Lee Williams, MA

Henry McGehee was a witness on the homestead application of my paternal great-grandfather, Randel Farnell.[123] He first appeared in the Suwannee County records when he married Jane Smiley on May 13, 1866.[124] On August 5, 1867, he registered to vote.[125] On September 21, 1869, he submitted application no. 4169 under the Homestead Act of 1862 in Tallahassee for a section of land located in the northeast quarter of the southwest quarter of section 12 in township 2L of range 13E, (Live Oak) equaling 39.89 acres.[126] The land was adjacent to my great-grandfather's.

According to the testimony of his two "disinterested" witnesses, Randel Farnell (my great-grandfather) and William Forsyth Bynum, deputy clerk of the Suwannee County Circuit Court, in the final proof, on the first day of January 1870, he built a "good dwelling house" that he and his wife, Jane, and four children, Adda, William, Ella and Lissie lived in. It was also noted that he had fenced and cultivated about fifteen to twenty acres. They went on to state that Henry had built a good log dwelling house, a corncrib and a smokehouse. They also noted that he had a good garden and had made other improvements.[127] Unfortunately, things did not go well for Henry when it came time to give his affidavit.

According to a petition given on Henry's behalf by friends and neighbors, he became seriously ill a few days after his witnesses testified. In addition, his wife became ill as well. It is possible they were suffering from malaria or yellow fever, which was a problem across mosquito-infested Florida. In any event, as a result, Henry was unable to travel to the land office in Gainesville, seventy miles away, and thus missed his deadline to make his final affidavit in support of his claim, resulting in the cancelation of the claim.[128]

Henry was still ill in November 1876, when twenty-nine friends and neighbors, including Randel Farnell, William Forsyth Bynum, the deputy clerk of the court, and Joseph Jacobs, Randel Farnell's brother-in-law and

Henry McGehee's homestead application. *Homestead Land Entry Papers, application no. 4169, NARA.*

Final Homestead Proof required under Section 2291 of the Revised Statutes of the United States.

WE, _Randall Farnall & W. F. Bynum Jr._ do solemnly _Swear_ that we have known _Henry McGehee_ for _Sixteen_ years last past; that he is _the head of a family_, consisting of _himself & his wife_ and _four children & he is_ a citizen of the United States; that he is an inhabitant of the _North East quarter of South West quarter_ of Section No. _Twelve_ in Township No. _Two South_ of Range No. _Thirteen E_, and that no other person resided upon the said land entitled to the right of Homestead or Pre-emption.

That the said _Henry McGehee_ entered upon and made settlement on said land on the _first_ day of _January_, 18_70_ and has built a house thereon _a good comfortable Log House with other improvements_

and has lived in the said house and made it his exclusive home from the _first_ day of _January_, 18_70_, to the present time, and that he has, since said settlement, plowed, fenced, and cultivated about _fifteen_ acres of said land, and has made the following improvements thereon, to wit: _A good Log Dwelling House — Corn Crib — Smoke House — good Garden & other improvements and with witness cause appeared the land & party named failure_

Randall X Farnall
W. F. Bynum Jr.

I, _William Forsyth Bynum_, do hereby certify that the above affidavit was taken and subscribed before me this _5th_ day of _May_, 18_77_, and that the parties are perfectly responsible—

Wm Forsyth Bynum Deft Clerk Circuit Court Suwannee County Fla.

I, _We certify_ that _Randall Farnall_ and _W. F. Bynum Jr._, whose names are subscribed to the foregoing affidavit, are persons of respectability.

Jo. H. Lee, Register.

_____, Receiver.

HOMESTEAD.

Land Office at _Gainesville Fla_
May 15th, 18_77_

FINAL CERTIFICATE, No. _1225_

APPLICATION, No. _4169_

It is hereby certified That, pursuant to the provisions of Section No. 2291, Revised Statutes of the United States, _Henry McGehee_, has made payment in full for _North East ¼ of South West ¼_

of Section No. _Twelve (12)_, in Township No. _Two (2) S._ of Range No. _Thirteen (13) E_, containing _thirtynine 89⁄100 (39 89⁄100)_ acres.

NOW, THEREFORE, BE IT KNOWN, That on presentation of this Certificate to the COMMISSIONER OF THE GENERAL LAND OFFICE, the said _Henry McGehee_ shall be entitled to a Patent for the Tract of Land above described.

Jo. H. Lee, Register.

Top: Final proof, homestead application. *Homestead Land Entry Papers, application no. 4169, NARA.*

Bottom: Henry McGehee's final certificate. *Homestead Land Entry Papers, application no. 1225, NARA.*

To the Hon. Commissioner of Lands
Washington D.C.

Honorable Sir – We the Subscribers Your Petitioners residing in Suwannee county State of Florida beg leave to represent to your Honor that one Henry McGehee a citizen of said county and State did on the 21st day of September 1869 at the Land Office in Tallahassee Florida made an Entry under the "Homestead Act," of the North East quarter of South West quarter of Section Twelve '12, in Township two '2, South of Range thirteen '13, East. and That said Henry McGehee did enter upon and made Settlement upon said Land on the first day of January 1870 that he built a good dwelling house thereon and has lived in said house from said 1st day of January 1870 and made it his exclusive home up to this date. Said McGehee has built other houses upon said Land and has fenced plowed and cultivated about fifteen or twenty acres. That the said Henry McGehee did on the Sixth day of September 1876 last by two responsible and disinterested Witnesses before the Clerk of the County Court of said county of Suwannee made under Oath with Seal of Clerks office attached his final proof of Actual Settlement and Cultivation of said Land as required by Section 2291 revised Statutes of the United States and That a few days thereafter said Henry McGehee was taken severely Sick and is yet Sick and Confined to his bed. So that it was quite

Henry McGehee's petition letter. *Homestead Land Entry Papers, application no. 4169, NARA.*

Sallie Jacobs Farnell, great-grandmother. *Courtesy of Margo Lee Williams.*

Henry's future son-in-law, petitioned the U.S. commissioner of lands to make an exception and allow Henry to provide his final testimony to the clerk of the court in Suwannee County.[129] On March 12, 1877, the commissioner authorized the homestead receiver's office in Tallahassee to reactivate Henry's application.[130] Then on May 5, 1877, Henry appeared before William Forsyth Bynum to make his final affidavit.[131] Randel Farnell and William Bynum's testimonies were also rewritten and certified again. Henry's final certificate, no. 1225, was issued on May 15, 1877.[132]

Unfortunately, Henry's wife, Jane, did not live to enjoy his victory. By the 1880 census, Henry was a widowed, a single father with four young children, Adda "Addie," William, Ella and Lissie.[133]

On October 4, 1884, Henry and one of the twenty-nine petitioners in his case, William Evans, testified on behalf of the homestead claim made by Randel Farnell.[134] On April 29, 1899, Henry's daughter Addie married his witness Joseph Jacobs, the youngest brother of Randel Farnell's wife, Sallie, and the son of another of Henry's petitioners, William Jacobs.[135]

Henry does not appear in the census after 1910.[136] It is presumed he died sometime before 1920 and was buried in Black City Cemetery, now located on private property behind Eastside Memorial Cemetery in Live Oak.

STEPHEN McCASKILL

By Orice Jenkins

Whitney Houston defied the odds each time she stood up to sing "The Greatest Love of All," but it was her great-grandfather who stood up to claim his rights as an American citizen nine decades earlier, treading the path for his progeny to follow.

Stephen McCaskill was born in April 1866 in Jackson County, Florida.[137] It is believed that he was the son of John Jett McCaskill, a white merchant, and Annie Hogan, a formerly enslaved Black woman. Stephen resided with his father as a child in Eucheeanna, Florida, and he is listed as a servant in the 1880 census.[138] He married Emma Houston of Pensacola, Florida, on

October 25, 1891.[139] They settled on their homesteaded land in November 1892, and Stephen submitted his homestead affidavit at the Walton County Clerk's Office in DeFuniak Springs, Florida, on November 19, 1894.

Stephen applied for the northeast quarter of section 24 in township 1, south of range 19, west of the Tallahassee principal meridian, but it was a mistake. He was living in the southwest quarter of section 23. He returned to the courthouse in March 1895 to correct his mistake and explain that someone had incorrectly told him the land numbers. After presenting witnesses and confirming that he had not mortgaged or sold any of the land, his application was corrected, and the homesteading process continued. Stephen testified during this ordeal that he had already cleared two acres and fenced them off. He signed all his affidavits with his name, proving that he could read and write.

Stephen returned to the courthouse in March 1900 to make his final proof. He made several improvements to the land, such as the addition of his house, a kitchen and a crib and stall for animals. By this time, Emma had given birth to three children: Nathaniel, Jamie and Eddie C.[140] They all lived consistently on the property after the house was built in November 1892. Stephen stated that on average, he had cultivated ten acres of land over the previous six seasons. His witnesses were two other homesteaders: Braxton Oates and Robert J. McKinnon.[141]

On March 9, 1900, Stephen received his final certificate. He received his land patent on April 9, 1901, signed by President William McKinley.[142] He officially owned 160.37 acres of land just outside of the Freeport, Florida city limit. By the time of the 1910 census, he was still listed as a landowner living near his homesteading brother-in-law, Joe Houston.[143] Stephen then had a fourth child, Adelia, but someone else was missing. Emma was gone, Stephen was recorded as widowed and his mother, Annie, was living with him, helping with the children.

Adelia, or Delia Mae, grew up to marry Nicholas "Nitch" Drinkard in Panama City, Florida.[144] She moved to his native Early County, Georgia, where they continued the legacy of landownership before fleeing north to Newark, New Jersey.[145] There, Delia gave birth to Emily Drinkard, known better as legendary vocalist Cissy Houston. This also makes Delia the grandmother of Whitney Houston and Dionne Warwick.

Near Nitch and Delia in Newark was the family of James and Emma Drinkard, Nitch's uncle and aunt.[146] More research led to the discovery of James's marriage license to Emma, in which her name is written "Emma Mcskell."[147] She was listed as a widow from Florida and the daughter of

Oliver and Rachel. Stephen McCaskill's in-laws were named Oliver and Rachel Houston. This 1926 marriage license for Nitch's uncle turned out to also be a marriage license for Delia's mother. She did not die, as indicated by Stephen McCaskill's 1910 census report, but she left him.

Stephen moved on as well, marrying Millie Lacy Campbell on November 29, 1920, in Walton County, Florida.[148] It was recorded in the 1930 census that he was with Millie as the owner of a home worth $200.[149] The value of the other houses on the page range from $50 to $500. Millie died from a stroke on October 13, 1936, actually leaving Stephen widowed this time. He was recorded as a retired homeowner in the 1940 census, with his nephew Calvin staying with him.[150] Calvin was also there in the 1945 Florida State census.[151]

Stephen died in 1954, outliving his daughter Delia and son-in-law Nitch Drinkard. His bountiful legacy spread far beyond the boundaries of Walton County, Florida. It is unlikely that he would've imagined the success of his descendants when he first submitted his homestead application in 1894, but his determination and intellect paved the way for his offspring to become global icons of the late twentieth century.

GEORGE JONES

By Deborah Mitchell

On January 28, 1891, George Jones filed a homestead entry for federal land (application no. 21095) under the Homestead Act of 1862 with the Gainesville, Florida Land Office.[152]

George Jones was born in South Carolina on September 15, 1846. His place of birth is listed as North Carolina in his application. However, U.S. census records for 1870, 1880 and 1900 say his place of birth is South Carolina.[153]

George Jones was thirty-four years old when enumerated in the June 1880 United States census. He and his wife, Caroline (Evans) Jones, lived in Old Store, Chesterfield, South Carolina, and were married for one year. George was listed as a farmer. Caroline was born in South Carolina in 1864 and listed in the census as a housekeeper. No children were listed. George and Caroline's first daughter, Bennie, was born later that year in November 1880. Over the next several years, five more children were born: Abe in 1882, Silas in 1885, Janie in 1886, Hattie in 1888 and Amos in 1891.

George solemnly swore in his application that he was a native-born citizen of the United States over the age of twenty-one who was the head of a family. George was forty-three years old, and his post office was located in LaCrosse, Florida. Although the 1880 U.S. census states that George was able to read and write, he signed his name with an X on all of the required documents.

George Jones applied for 40.05 acres of land in LaCrosse, Florida, specifically the southwest quarter of the southeast quarter of section 20, in township 7 south of range 19 east of the Tallahassee meridian in Florida and paid the required $6 filing fee. George settled the land in April 1891 and moved his family to LaCrosse in the summer of 1893. The improvements made to the land included the addition of a log dwelling house, a kitchen, a corncrib (a barn-type structure used to store corn), fencing and trees. He valued his homestead at about $200. Over the next several years, three more children were born: Edgar in 1893, Phillip in 1895 and John in 1896. George continued to cultivate the land and lived continuously in his home with his family.

On February 3, 1896, George returned to the Gainesville Land Office. There, he asserted before register J.M. Barco and receiver N.D. Wainwright that he would present final proof to establish his cultivation and residence on his homestead.

On April 2, 1896, public notice of the homestead application appeared in the *Gainesville Weekly SUN*, a newspaper published in the city of Gainesville, Alachua County. The notice was published for six weeks preceding April 2, 1896. The posting was attested to by land office register J.M. Barco, who also certified that a printed copy of the notice was posted in a conspicuous place in his office for thirty days beginning on February 3, 1896.

On April 2, 1896, George appeared before land office register N.D. Wainwright and solemnly swore in his final affidavit that he had cultivated and resided on the land since April 1891.

Four men were listed as witnesses in George's application, namely Willis Turner and Sam Burnett (also homesteaders in the area), Tas. Bloodworth and Dick Beckam, all from LaCrosse, Florida. Dick Beckam and Tas. Bloodworth appeared with George to provide witness testimony in support of his application. Both testimonies were similar. Beckam and Bloodworth testified that: (1) George had settled on the land for about five and a half years; (2) George built a dwelling house, a kitchen and a corncrib; (3) George and his family had resided on the homestead continuously since his first settlement and had not been absent from the property; (4) fifteen acres of

Final Certificate No. _13725_

Homestead Application No. _21095_

_O. K._

LAND OFFICE

AT

Gainesville, Fla.

April 7, 18_96_

Sect. _20_, Town. _7 S_, Range _19 E_

Div. C, List No. 44

Approved _July 7_ 18_96_

J. C. Patton Clerk,

_JC_

Division

Patented _July 27,_ 18_96_

Recorded, Vol. _25_, page _83_

_A. 6/222_

George Jones land approval, cover for Homestead Land Entry Papers, application no. 21095 and patent no. 12225, NARA.

the land was cultivated producing four crops, the fifth crop was planted; (5) there was no oil or other minerals present and that the land was more valuable as agricultural land than for its mineral potential; (6) the property had not been mortgaged; (7) neither had a vested interest in the property; and (8) improvements made to the property was valued at about $200. Both witnesses signed their name with the mark of an X on their final proof document.

On July 27, 1896, George Jones was issued patent no. 12225 for 40.05 acres of land located in LaCrosse, Alachua County, Florida. Twenty-four years after settling on his homestead in 1891, George died on July 15, 1915, at the age of sixty-eight. Caroline died in 1935 at the age of seventy. George and Caroline had been married for thirty-five years.

Upon George's death, the ownership of the homestead was moved to his son Silas Jones. Silas and his first wife, Rosetta Parker Jones, had five children: Frank, Araminta "Orrie," Albert, Australia and Leroy. Rosetta died on July 15, 1914, in LaCrosse, Alachua County, Florida, when she was thirty years old. Three years later, Silas married Julia Thelma Lawson Jones on June 24, 1917.[154] They had ten children: George, Victoria, Daisy, Theresa "Teress," Samuel, Joseph, Ernest, Naomi, Julia Carolyn, Betty and one adopted daughter, Ida Pearl.

Silas and Julia lived and worked on the family farm for their entire lives, as did their children until they all left home to start their own families. Silas and Julia served at Bethel AME Church and remained faithful members for fifty-two years. Silas served as the leader of Class Number One for forty-six years. His favorite saying was: "It's not what you make, but what you save." Julia was a strong, hardworking woman who could outwork anyone in the fields. She also worked for the church selling peanuts, ice cream and candy for fifteen years to help build a new church. Julia loved her family and adored her church, community and friends. She later became a speaker/evangelist.

Above: The second Jones family home, built in 1891 by George Jones. *Courtesy of Deborah Mitchell.*

Left: Silas Emanuel Jones (the grandson of Silas) visits the family homestead in January 2022. *Courtesy of Deborah Mitchell.*

Silas and Julia's grandsons Silas Emanuel and Phillip were raised by their grandparents and lived in the second Jones family home built on the homestead. Daisy Jones was their mother. After the Jones children had all left home, Silas Emanuel and Phillip helped their grandparents farm the land, working incessantly to keep up with the daily demands of the farm. Silas Emanuel and Phillip lived and worked on the farm until they graduated from high school in 1958 and 1959, respectively.

Each year, the land yielded crops of corn, string beans, cucumber, bell pepper, peas, squash, sugar cane, greens and tobacco. Two horses named Molly and Rudy were used to pull the cultivating plows. Tractors and other farm equipment were utilized in the day-to-day operations of the farm. There was livestock, such as cows, hogs, chickens, roosters and a few goats.

Of all of George Jones's children, his son Silas lived on the homestead for over eighty years. He died in Jacksonville, Duval, Florida, on August 15, 1970, around the age of eighty-five. (The Florida U.S. Death Index records his year of birth as 1889 and the Find a Grave index records his year of birth as 1885.)[155] Silas's wife, Julia, died on September 20, 1968, in Alachua, Florida, when she was seventy-two years old. Silas and Julia are buried at Newnansville African American Cemetery in Alachua, Alachua County, Florida, along with other Jones family members. They had been married for fifty-one years.

Upon Silas's death, ownership of the homestead was moved to his eldest son, George L. Jones. George died at the age of seventy-two on May 22, 1990. Upon George L. Jones's death, the ownership moved to three of his fourteen children, one of whom, Jerry Jones, died in 2001.

Remarkably, for over 131 years, the 40.05 acres of land that Florida homesteader George Jones worked so hard to obtain in 1891 has remained in the family. The extraordinary efforts of the Jones family to carry on the legacy of their ancestors is one that future generations can certainly be proud of.

CONTRIBUTOR: *Deborah A. Mitchell is the daughter of Silas Emanuel Jones, who is the grandson of Silas Jones and great-grandson of George Jones. The homesteading history of George Jones was written in collaboration with Silas Emanuel Jones.*

4

LOUISIANA BLACK
HOMESTEADERS

You may encounter many defeats, but you must not be defeated. In fact, it may be
necessary to encounter the defeats so you can know who you are, what you can rise
from, how you can still come out of it.
—Maya Angelou

The Homestead National Historical Park Service documented 22, 988 homesteads in Louisiana out of a total of 27,882,240 acreages, and this translated to 9 percent of land acquired out of the total 2,561, 334 acreages available.

The landowners in this chapter are from nine parishes—Ascension, Bossier, East Baton Rouge, East Feliciana, Livingston, St. Helena, Washington, West Feliciana and Claiborne. Some descendants were aware of landownership, and others discovered this land through searching the Bureau of Land Management for the land patent certificates. Upon making this discovery, they obtained their land entry papers and summarized the findings.

In this chapter, readers will learn about formerly enslaved men and women and their journeys to land ownership. Also, some of these settlers were former members of United States Colored Troops. Regardless of their status, they traveled to land offices in New Orleans, East Baton Rouge and Natchitoches to apply and successfully acquire land between 1870 and 1930.

CHARLES BAPTISTE

By Bernice A. Bennett

I learned about Charles Baptiste when I found his name in the family Bible. My mother informed me that he was a close friend to our family. Upon further investigation, I noticed in the 1880 U.S. census that he was living in Maurepas, Louisiana, near my great-great-great-grandfather Thomas Youngblood.[156] I also discovered that Charles served as a witness for my great-great-grandfather Peter Clark's homestead application, no. 9590, and as a witness for my grandmother's marriage in 1913.[157] Clovis Russell, the nephew of Charles, married Peter Clark's daughter, Dollie Clark. With this information, I decided to further explore information about Charles Baptiste.

Charles Baptiste was born around 1857 in Maurepas, Louisiana, to John and Matilda Baptiste. I learned about the Baptiste family from a Freedman Bank and Trust record filed by Charles's half-sibling, Joseph Colbert.[158] In addition to Joseph, Charles had three other siblings: Peter, Jane (Baptiste) Russell Doughty and Delphine (Baptiste) Vidal. Charles's half-brother Joseph was a Stevedore in New Orleans, his sister Delphine was a schoolteacher and his brother Peter Baptice (note the spelling of his last name) also became a homesteader.[159]

When he was thirty-five years old, on August 11, 1887, Charles Baptiste filed application no. 9844 for 120.44 acres of land in Livingston Parish, Louisiana.[160] His house was located on "his original farm that was built twenty years earlier." The house consisted of two rooms and a kitchen. The homestead had one well, fencing, a chicken house, a crib, fruit trees, a garden and "about seven to eight acres fenced on his original and adjoining farm" valued at $500.

Baptiste listed Ovide Alexis (also a homesteader), M.F. Bradford, Mark Harris and Adrien Vidal (also a homesteader) as witnesses to his claim.[161]

Charles Baptiste was a part of a community of Black homesteaders in Livingston Parish, Louisiana. He received his land patent, no. 5274, for his 120.44 acres of land on January 22, 1895.

Baptiste never married, as his mother was dependent on him and resided on the homestead with him. He lived on this land for twenty years.

In 1911, Baptiste sold six acres of his land for $150 to the School Board of Livingston Parish to create a schoolhouse that improved the quality of the public education in the area.

CONTRIBUTOR: *Bernice Alexander Bennett is an award winning author, genealogist and family researcher.*

PETER CLARK

By Bernice A. Bennett

According to my family Bible records, Peter Clark was born on January 31, 1855, in St. Helena Parish, Louisiana.[162] Because of the American Civil War, his childhood was a time of transition, and he saw freedom differently than his parents.

Peter is first found in federal records from April 1868 on the Coxe Plantation in Livingston Parish; there, he lived with his mother, Katie Clark, and siblings Ann, Olivia, Hester, Emma and Bob. The plantation owners, William P. Coxe, Benjamin F. Coxe, John B. Easterly and R.C. Webb, negotiated a labor contract to pay Katie and her family one hundred dollars per annum to perform duties on the plantation. In addition to the Clark family, Bob Lee, Solomon Goss and Elie Johnson were employed to receive ten dollars per month for their services.[163]

In 1870, Peter's surname was listed as Johnson, yet his surname was always Clark, as noted in the Freedmen's Bureau Labor contract.[164] Peter's surname was also Clark in the later 1880 U.S. census, and he is documented as marrying Rebecca Youngblood in 1874 in St. Helena Parish.[165]

According to U.S. census data, Peter worked as a farmhand in 1870 and as a laborer in 1880 to support his wife and two young children.[166] In 1887, he applied for public land in Livingston Parish under the Homestead Act of 1862.

Peter's father-in-law and the father of Rebecca Youngblood Clark, Thomas Youngblood, owned a small farm in Livingston Parish, as noted in the 1870 and 1880 U.S. censuses.[167] Upon Thomas Youngblood's death in 1882, succession records proved that he also owned land; however, information about how he acquired this land was not given in the court papers.[168]

As noted previously, Peter Clark applied on October 15, 1887, for 159.33 acres of land under the Homestead Act of 1862. The land was located in the town of Maurepas in Livingston Parish, Louisiana, at the southeastern quarter of the northwest half and the eastern half of the southwest quarter, and the northwestern quarter of the southwest quarter of section 2 TP.9S.R.5E southeast. It was described as piney woods, and once cleared, it could be good for planting crops.[169]

Peter Clark cleared five of the 159.33 acres of land to build a house and an outhouse and grow an assortment of crops to sustain and support his family. He had a network of family and friends to serve as witnesses to

Opposite: A photograph of Peter Clark with his son Moses Clark, circa 1906. *Courtesy of Bernice A. Bennett.*

Above: The Homestead Land Patent for Peter Clark. *Original copy courtesy of Bernice A. Bennett.*

testify that he lived on the land as required by the Homestead Act. Many of those witnesses were also close neighbors of Peter's father-in-law, Thomas Youngblood, who died in 1882, leaving a small estate to his family.[170]

On October 15, 1895, Peter did submit proof to the land office in New Orleans that he had complied with the homesteader's rules for settlers. He asked the following individuals to serve as witnesses to testify on his behalf: Charles Baptiste (also a homesteader), Henry Tinkshell (also a homesteader), Marshall Douglas, Alfred Robinson (also a homesteader) and Ida and Robert Benefield (also a homesteader). In compliance with the Homestead Act, the *Southland* newspaper published a notice for six consecutive weeks beginning on October 17, 1894, to ensure that the entire community knew that Peter was in the final process of officially acquiring his land.[171]

Peter noted in his final application that his house was built and that he had established an actual residence on the land more than ten years ago. He added a dwelling valued at $50, an outhouse for $5, fenced and cleared five acres for $50, bringing the land's total value to $105. He also cultivated about five acres for ten years.

His family included his wife and four children, and they lived on the land continuously after first establishing residence.

Although Peter answered the required questions, he almost missed the final filing date because he had difficulty raising the money to pay for his transportation to New Orleans and other expenses. He pleaded his case as documented in his land entry application file, no. 9590:

> *Before me, the undersigned authority, personally came and appeared Peter Clark, who being by me first duly sworn, deposes and says that he is the identical person who made Homestead Entry no. 9590 on April 25, 1887; that the seven years in which homesteaders are required to make proof in support of their entries expired in his case on April 25, 1894, and his final proof made this day in support of his said entry no. 9590 is not within the statutory period. That he is a very poor man and that until today he has not been able to get money to pay the cost of making proof, and this is the earliest day he had the money. That he has lived on and cultivated his land in good faith for over ten years, and it would work a great hardship were he deprived of his entry. Wherefore, he prays that his Proof be accepted passed, his final certificate receipt issued and thereon that he may receive patent on his said entry after the necessary formalities in the provisos.*
>
> *Sworn to and subscribed,*
> *Peter x Clark*
> [his mark]
> *Before me A.D. 1894 G. Mc Brumby, register*

In 1896, once he had pleaded his case, Peter Clark received his homestead land patent certificate, no. 5887, and by the 1900 U.S. census, he was listed as a farmer residing on the land with his wife, two children and two grandchildren.[172] Peter Clark died as a farmer and landowner in 1909 in New Orleans at the age of fifty-five.[173]

CONTRIBUTOR: *Bernice Alexander Bennett is the great-great-granddaughter of Peter Clark.*

PHOEBE ANN BARTLETT FRANKLIN

By Kimberli Hornes

Phoebe Ann (Bartlett) Franklin is my maternal great-great-grandmother whose story I am beyond honored and privileged to share.

Wealthy banker and slaveowner William J. Minor revealed in his "List of Negroes" diary (housed at Louisiana State University) that Phoebe (Bartlett) Franklin was born to Frederick and Molly Bartlett on March 10, 1835, at his Waterloo Plantation in Geismar, Ascension Parish, Louisiana. She was enslaved there until she was emancipated.

She married Shedrick "Shed" Franklin Sr. when they were both enslaved on the same plantation. They were the parents of nine children, Amy, Minty, Betsy, Moses, Corrine, Shedrick, Louisa and Willie. Their daughter Edy died in birth in December 1856, and Shedrick Franklin Sr. passed away in August 1885.

Phoebe Franklin filed her homestead application, no. 13822, on March 10, 1892. However, she and her husband may have settled on the land earlier, since he was listed as a farmer in the 1870 U.S. census. They established continuous residency in 1874, cultivating six acres containing a small "shanty" house, a corn crib, a cotton house and an outhouse, all valued at one hundred dollars.

As the head of her household, Phoebe and her two youngest children, Louisa (about ten years of age) and Willie (about nine years of age), resided with her at the time that she initiated her application.

Phoebe could not read or write, and her application reveals that she signed her documentation by marking an X. Her witnesses were her neighbors Moses Bureau (also a homesteader), James Banks, Edmund Jackson and George Roberson. The most astounding thing to me is that these four men, in the year 1892, were collectively willing to assist and support a woman in such a lucrative, personal endeavor.

Phoebe Franklin received her homestead patent, no. 5937, for 42.23 acres of land on April 11, 1896. By that time, she had already cultivated four additional acres of land (up to ten acres).

Acquiring this land felt unprecedented for a Black woman in the Deep South. As I researched this land by studying maps, it appears as if it was once the property of Phoebe's former enslaver, William J. Minor, and the Waterloo Plantation where she was enslaved. This could explain how the land was accessible to her for cultivation. A respected elder historian at

Left: Doris Ludora Walker Bellamy, maternal grandmother. *Right*: Corrine Franklin Walker (1869–1952), maternal great-grandmother. *Courtesy of Kimberli Hornes.*

William Minor's Southdown Plantation in Houma, Louisiana, stated that Minor would grant his enslaved people specific areas on his land (at his various plantations) to produce their own crops. Little did he know the effect this would have.

I am so proud of my great-great-grandmother Phoebe Franklin and her industriousness and steadfast attitude that has been handed down throughout the generations to the daughters of her maternal line. A formerly enslaved woman did not allow anything to hinder her from pursuing an opportunity that could benefit her and her offspring for years to come.

In 1920, my great-uncle Shed led the family in migrating to Detroit, Michigan. This included his mother, my great-grandmother Corrine (Phoebe's daughter) and her children, my then-seventeen-year-old grandmother Doris, great-uncle Sandy, great-uncle Richard and their baby sister, Montana (Nancy). I had the pleasure of having all these relatives (except for Grandma Corrine and Aunt Nancy) in my life to assist in nurturing and raising me. I am proud to say that my mother and I were born and raised there in a loving, warm and thriving environment.

Phoebe Franklin sold over ten acres of her land soon after acquiring it, and in September 1944, her two surviving daughters, my great-grandmother Corrine and her sister Louisa, and their deceased siblings' offspring received full ownership of her property (she had already passed away). In May 1968, Phoebe's grandchildren sold the remaining acres of her land to Wilfred Duplessis of Geismar, Ascension Parrish.

My mother remembers my grandmother Doris (whom I fondly called Nana), receiving the aforementioned documentation at our home in Detroit in 1968, before my birth. Mr. Duplessis later sold it to land developer Cheri McDaniel, who acquired the land in 1977 and created a home development called Vista Del Lago. She has since sold it.

Phoebe Franklin's land is located off the I-10 Freeway, halfway between New Orleans and Baton Rouge in Dutch Town, Ascension Parish, Louisiana (the Gonzales, Louisiana area). When exiting Highway 429 for Dutch Town going west, you make a left on 429, take the road all the way around, traveling from Kings Road to Shadow Lake Drive, to behold all that was once bestowed upon Phoebe. Traveling alone, I had the opportunity to visit what I will forever refer to as her land in 2018. I exited my rental car and just stood there, staring at the beautiful, lush greenery that still exists, imagining her gleefully walking her beautiful acreage, knowing that she and my great-great-grandfather Shed were once dwelling in its midst. I sentimentally wished they were still there, emancipated and thriving.

We lovingly thank and honor our great-grand matriarch, Phoebe Ann Bartlett Franklin. Because she existed and, most importantly, endured, we are here. She has influenced me to say, "Oh, yes, I can! Watch me! Especially if my God be willing!"

CONTRIBUTOR: *Kimberli Hornes (and on behalf of her beloved mama, Joyce) contributed this story. Kimberli is the maternal great-great-granddaughter of Phoebe Ann Bartlett Franklin (Phoebe > Corrine > Doris > Joyce > Kimberli). She enjoys taking a "sentimental journey home" by way of consistently indulging in personal genealogical research.*

FRANK THOMPSON

By Dr. Dolores Mercedes Franklin

Frank Thompson, Davy and Sally Franklin Thompson's son was a Louisiana homesteader who settled on contested land in Ascension Parish's New River settlement. His family endured unjust evictions in the *Crossley v. Reed* lawsuit. Frank withstood legal battles until the diabolical campaign of

Picard and Geismar exploited his children. Frank had tenacity, keeping his land for forty years and surviving the ordeal. His wealth, though minimal, was passed to his heirs.

In 1872, Frank Thompson settled on "public land" in Ascension Parish. He submitted Homestead Land Application no. 13841 on April 11, 1892. Frank filed for 40.32 acres in Section 27 in the New River settlement on the Riverside Plantation plot on the rear border adjoining Waterloo Plantation, where his family had been enslaved. He met the requirements under the Homestead Act of 1862, having settled continuously for twenty years.[174]

Frank's experience delayed his land application with a lawsuit that threatened the legitimacy of his claim. On March 3, 1884, the U.S. Supreme Court's decision on the Houmas Land Claim resolved the long-standing dispute over the vast contested New River territory but required enabling legislation. In the court's opinion, "The Houmas Grant is famous in the history of land titles in Louisiana." A centuries-old tale was unfolding where Frank's family had settled in the rear of the Waterloo and Riverside Plantations fronting the Mississippi River. The Houmas Land Claim, a land title lawsuit, contested the rear boundaries. A Houma chief traded all the land east of the Mississippi River in a "supposed land sale." The land was a source of conflict. From 1808, this dispute was huge, involving land speculators and fraudulent claims, setting the stage for Frank's fears into the twentieth century.

The homesteads were in the rear of riverfront plantations represented as New River Landing. Lines fanning out from the back of the Houma Village approximate the borders of the claim limits, the contested rear borders of plantations.[175]

Within days of the supreme court's decision, a lawsuit against Black settlers was announced: *Crossley and Sons v. Saul Reed et al.* Crossley was the riverfront owner in the Houmas Claim and the owner of three plantations (Riverside, Mount Houmas and Southwood). Crossley's suit was filed against persons occupying the rear lands commonly designated as "public lands." Crossley claimed to hold government patents and charged the defendants— the settlers in the rear Riverside plot, including the land behind Waterloo— with trespassing, threatening Frank's homestead claim.

The contested New River territory opened for homestead entry in 1889 with the passage of the Gay Bill, an act that enabled the claims of homesteaders after the 1884 supreme court decision in the Houmas Land Claim case. It restored to the public domain certain lands in New River territory.

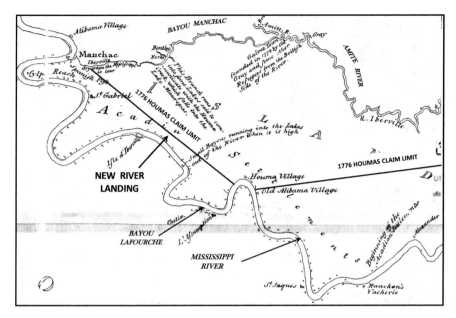

The family homesteads and contested boundaries in Houmas Land Claim decided by the U.S. Supreme Court. *Detail of George Gauld's* 1778 A Plan of the Coast of Part of West Florida and Louisiana, *adapted 2022, D.M. Franklin.*

In January 1890, Judge Billings published the Crossley case decision, a decree ordering *that the plaintiffs in* the *Crossley case take possession of the contested land, resulting in* the mass eviction of Black settlers. Frank's family was listed in the decree by either name or section number. Assured by officials in 1868 that rear lands were public, settlers believed in the promise of reconstruction: that court decisions would apply equally to them. Knowing that eviction meant losing everything, Billings refused a rehearing requested by Black homesteaders, then empowered by the facts.

Arthur Burnett pleaded in an interview, "The Houmas Tract: A Talk with One of the Settlers About to be Evicted," on January 16, 1890, in the *Times-Democrat*:

> *I do not think that any community exists in the world which would not sympathize with us in the misfortune that has come to us. It seems indeed hard that after twenty years of industry through sickness, bad crops years and all the discouragements attending opening new lands and paying debts, taxes and expenses, that without any equivalent, we must surrender everything that men hold dear. I am one of those who have been settled there since 1869.*

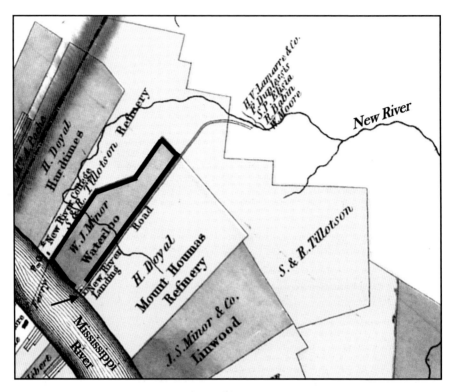

Contested rear lands riverfront plantations and contested rear public lands in legal battles. *Crossley v. Reed* (1884): Waterloo Plantation was bounded above and in the rear by R.&S. Tillotson (then the Riverside Plantation) and below by Mount Houmas Plantation. Hardtimes Plantation (then the Southwood Plantation). *Detail of George Gauld's* 1778 A Plan of the Coast of Part of West Florida and Louisiana, *adapted 2022, D.M. Franklin.*

In February 1890, a marshal and armed deputies came to execute the court order. Frank's family listed in the degree signed a statement relinquishing land claims. They paid rent to Ellis, the successive owner, to avoid physical removal—either that or did not leave.

There were few winners among the Crossley evictees with restitution for their seized homesteads. Officials wrote the words "Act March 2, 1889, Gay Bill" on Frank's homestead application, showing that his land met the provisions of the bill: judged "public land." Frank and his two brothers became homesteaders, while the husbands of Sally's daughters suffered the misfortune of losing their homesteads, years of hard labor and all their improvements.

Frank persevered. On April 15, 1893, attested by Leon Picard, he signed the notice of intention to make final proof on June 10, 1893, with an X. Frank's brother Edward and H.R. Butler gave testimony. Frank testified

THE HOUMAS GRANT

MANY SETTLERS THEATENED WITH EVICTION.
Unless They Can Get a Stay of Proceedings
They Will Be Expelled from Their Homes by Federal Power

Some Fear That Serious Trouble will Result.

... It is estimated that there are more than 1000 settlers upon the tracts of land lying back of the three plantations. They have been settled for 20 years or more, and in some cases as high as 100 acres is cultivated by one settler. The improvements consist of sugar houses, cotton gins and farm dwellings. The shipments of cotton from the territory occupied by the squatters amounting to 3000 bales, a great quantity of sugar and other products.

The negroes who were tempted to take up these lands did so from the impressions conceived in the general confusion arising out of

THE HOUMAS GRANT

... one of the defendants possesses a $3000 sugar house and cultivates nearly 100 acres.

A. Burnett, one of those seen in the Circuit Court Saturday, tills twenty-eight acres, Milton Morris 160 acres and Bart Willard sixty-nine acres. Each one of these claim that the United States Surveyor General told them in 1868 that all land except the eighty arpents front was government land. They had settled upon the land since 1866, had fenced and ditched it, worked knee deep in water to get their homes and to-day, after having bought lumber, bricks and provisions from the Crossleys, were to be turned out. Wellard produced several receipted bills headed, Crossley's Plantation Store, dated in 1868, and said they had encouraged people to settle upon the lands as government lands, and credited them with provisions that they could live on.

The Houmas Grant. Many settlers were threatened with eviction. *From the Times-Democrat (New Orleans), January 14, 1890.*

that he had a wife, seven children and sixteen acres of land cleared and in cultivation. He cultivated crops on twelve acres for the past twenty years and valued his property at $500. He built his house and established residence in 1873, and his improvements included a horse stable, a barn and fencing. Frank received Homestead Patent no. 4814 on March 27, 1895.

Threatening the legitimacy of Frank's patent, the riverfront planters and successor owners continued to contest the boundaries of Waterloo, Riverside and public lands in legal battles into the twentieth century. In 1903, Frank's section 27 was the subject of *Ellis v. Crossley*. Ellis bought the three plantations in 1888 from Crossley, who sold the land under full warranty and limited warranty—let the buyer beware.

The judge found his decision difficult because the maps for section 27 were inconsistent with the descriptions of the tracts. He sided with Ellis and said that Crossley sold warranted land, part of the Riverside Plantation, that was occupied by Frank's neighbors, Black homesteaders with patents, but the judge recognized that section 27 also contained public land. The court assessed the damage for the breach of the warranty at $1,300 rather than eject patent holders.

In 1911, Picard and Geismar (P&G) focused on Frank. P&G bought the homesteaded lands of Frank's Black neighbors on two to three sides of his property. Frank's land was strategically positioned at the major land transportation route that ran through section 27. It was near the road's intersection with New River. Section 27 adjoined the rear border of Waterloo about midway between Picard's store, at Dutchtown and the Mississippi River.

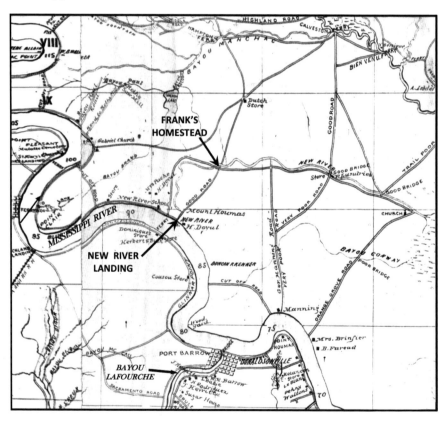

The strategic location of Frank Thompson's Homestead in New River Territory. *Detail of Henry L. Abbot's 1863 Department of the Gulf Map No. 2: New Orleans to Vicksburg, which was created at the time of the enactment of the Homestead Act of 1862; adapted 2022, D.M. Franklin.*

A campaign to encourage Frank to give up his homestead began when P&G enticed Frank's son Mike in November 1911 with a large payment of seventy-five dollars, convincing him that since his mother, Frank's first wife, died and never had a succession, he was due the amount from his mother's side in exchange for the deed to his one-fourteenth share of the land.

In January 1912, Frank filed a division of his property. As the surviving spouse, he inherited one-half and sold half to his heirs, including his children and grandchildren, for $400. In February, Frank advertised his half for sale as twenty acres of choice cane land with improvements for $1,500.

Picard and Geismar v. Frank Thompson et al. was filed. In November 1912, Frank pleaded to the court for half of his land with improvements because he lived there. To force a partition, the court recognized his first wife in the community as the owner in her own right to one-half of the homestead patent. While Frank could not sell his divided half interest, P&G enticed his daughter to deed them her undivided shares of one-seventh of the half of the property for $40.32 by using the same strategy that worked with Mike.

Frank did not pay taxes in 1914. Frank sold his undivided one-half to P&G for $200 in January 1915. By court order, the property was auctioned at a sheriff's sale. P&G, the only bidder, bought the land for $300. After court costs, $160.35 was distributed. P&G, with nine-fourteenths of the shares received $103.08. Frank's children each received $11.45, and grandchildren received one-third of $11.45. Combined, Frank's heirs inherited $57.25 from the sale. The five tutors received a total of $50.00.

Frank lived to see his son Mike acquire a land patent in 1929, thereby becoming a landowner. He died a widower in 1932 in Ascension Parish at the age of eighty-two. The older generation before Frank had started the chain of family members who owned land. Whether they won or lost their homesteads, the fact that Sally's sons and two generations of the family remained unified by high aspirations of land ownership was an accomplishment.

CONTRIBUTOR: *Dr. Dolores Mercedes Franklin is the great-granddaughter of William "Bill" Franklin, the family's iconic first landowner. He was the brother of Shedwick Franklin and Sally Franklin Thompson, the mother of Edward, Isaac and Frank. Franklin gratefully acknowledges her cousin Brianna Riley, a direct descendant of Sally Franklin Thompson's daughter Phyliss Thompson; and Kathe Hambrick, the founder of the River Road African American Museum (RRAAM) in Donaldsonville, Louisiana.*

THOMAS MONROE PITTMAN

By Marilyn Stubblefield

Thomas M. Pittman was born around 1865 in Mitch, Louisiana, which is and was a predominately Black community in Bogalusa, Louisiana.[176] Although his exact date of birth is unknown, his death certificate indicates that he died on February 9, 1943, at the age of seventy-eight. He was married to his third wife, Stella Pittman, at the time of death.

Although his original homestead application, no. 20321, was received and filed on July 12, 1899, he canceled his application on September 10, 1903, through a relinquishment filed in the New Orleans General Land Grant Office. On October 9 of the same year, Thomas Pittman transmitted a sworn statement to request that his application be reinstated, slightly less than a month after canceling. His initial request to cancel the application came about due to threats from certain white people, which was corroborated by W. Thomas McElroy through an affidavit. Friends advised him to withdraw his application for fear of his safety, even though his father, Wade Pittman, had acquired 158.82 acres of land the same way with his land entry application, no. 7570, in September 1883.

At the time of his application, Tom was married with three children. His wife was the former Etta Dillon (per vital check records, they were married on November 9, 1899), and his three children at the time of his application were Willie Pittman, John Wesley Pittman and my great-grandmother Alma Jane Pittman, born, in 1900, 1902 and 1903, respectively. Tom had five more children with Etta between 1905 to 1913. Their names were Rosa, Lucious, Julia, Pearl and Ollie Mae.

On July 18, 1904, a notice was submitted to the *Franklinton New Era* newspaper in Franklinton, Louisiana, announcing Thomas Pittman's intention to make final proof in support of his claim to obtain his land. In compliance with the law, a printed copy of the editor's certificate of publication was published weekly for no less than thirty days from July 30, 1904, to September 2, 1904. It was also posted on the wall in the land office in New Orleans for that same period.

Some two months later, on September 20, 1904, before the clerk of Franklinton, Louisiana, Pittman had the following witnesses prove his continuous residence upon the cultivation of the land: Albire John, Nathan Bruns, Wilmot Cooper and W.H. McGehee, all of Washington Parish.

Thomas
Pittman and
Etta Dillon.
*Courtesy
of Marilyn
Stubblefield.*

He also submitted his final affidavit required of homestead claimants, in which he swore that he made an actual settlement on the land, cultivated the land and had resided there since 1899. He also swore that no part of the land had been alienated and that he was the sole bona fide owner as an actual settler on April 4, 1905. His application indicates that he used about three acres to raise crops for five seasons and that there was a dwelling house, a crib, a field and fencing valued at $150. His required notice of application/land grant was approved on April 22, 1905, and patented on May 7, 1905. It was recorded in volume 15, page 362 for 121.95 acres of land in St. Helena Principal Meridian.

CONTRIBUTOR: *Marilyn Stubblefield is the great-great-granddaughter of Thomas M. Pittman and Etta Dillon.*

WADE PITTMAN

By Marilyn Stubblefield

Wade Pittman was born in April 1848, in Columbia, Marion County, Mississippi. At the age of forty-five, in July 1883, Wade Pittman of Lees Creek, Louisiana, settled on his land. By August of that year, he established his residence and built a dwelling house of pine logs, an eighteen-by-twenty-foot kitchen, a smokehouse, a corn crib and a stable valued at one hundred dollars.

Wade Pittman submitted his land entry application, no. 7570, on September 25, 1883, at the New Orleans Land Office for 158.82 acres of land located in Washington Parish, Louisiana.[177]

He cleared and cultivated twelve acres for seven seasons for farming and agricultural purposes.

At the time of his application, Wade had a wife, Eliza Jane (Tyson, sometimes spelled Tison) Pittman, and had the following children, as noted in the 1900 U.S. census, Amada Pittman, Lacyse Pittman, Abram Pittman, Samuel Pittman, Laura Pittman, Isabell Pittman, Perdie Pittman, Elijah Pittman, Merida Pittman, Susan Pittman and Hubert Pittman.[178] The couple had a total of fifteen children, including their eldest son, Thomas Monroe Pittman.

In compliance with the homestead guidelines, Wade named two witnesses to testify on his behalf, Gus Dean (thirty) and William Morris (twenty-one), both from Lee's Creek, Louisiana. These men supported Wade's testimony concerning the improvements and length of time he had established an actual residence on the property.[179]

In addition, a notice was placed in the *New Era* newspaper in Franklinton, Louisiana, on December 31, 1894, notifying the community of Wade's final steps to become a landowner. That newspaper named Gus Dean, William Morris and John T. Childs as witnesses.

Twelve years and one day later, Wade's application was approved on September 26, 1895, and twenty-seven days after that, he received approval for his homestead patent certificate, no. 5577, on October 23, 1895.[180]

Wade mentioned in his land application that he had a smokehouse, and he passed this tradition of smoking meat on to his descendants. To this day, a wild hog is smoked for the annual family reunion on the same plot land by his descendants. Thomas Pittman, one of Wade's sons, also received a homestead land patent, no. 12085, on May 9, 1905, in the area known today as Bogalusa, Mitch, Louisiana. Family input claims that the community of Mitch, Bogalusa, was named by the Pittmans and that many descendants either still live on or own land in that community.

CONTRIBUTOR: *Marilyn Stubblefield is the great-great-great-granddaughter of Wade Pittman, and her story is based on records found through an internet search, original land entry papers and information passed down from the descendants of Wade Pittman.*

GEORGE PAYSINGER

By Felix Scott Jr.

George Paysinger made his settlement in Bossier Parish, Louisiana, in December 1874, several years after emancipation.

George established an actual residence on the property on January 24, 1875, when he completed Homestead Entry no. 1039 at the Natchitoches, Louisiana Land Office under the Homestead Act of 1862. George fulfilled all of the requirements, including building a house and living on the land, to receive a patent on August 3, 1882. The 160.6-acre parcel was located just east of Plain Dealing, Louisiana, and ran north toward the Arkansas border.

George was a master architect, builder, craftsman and farmer. Among the many achievements in his life, George, as a formerly enslaved person, served as a juror for the second judicial court in Bossier Parish on April 3, 1882. During the years in which homesteaders were required to make proof in support of their entries, George Paysinger, his wife and five children made numerous improvements to the property. They cleared and fenced about fifteen acres and constructed two cabins for residences, a smokehouse, a corn crib, a cotton house and a wagon shelter. In addition, ten acres were cleared, where they grew cotton and corn. George had neighbors with whom he had close relationships for over twenty years, some during his enslavement.

Several of George's neighbors and longtime acquaintances agreed to serve as the required witnesses to testify for his homestead entry. Cornelius Howell and Henry C. Wyche completed the two witness testimony statements. S.C. O'Daniel, R.E. Wyche, J.N. Bryan, Ernest Wyche and at least one other also agreed to serve as witnesses on February 10, 1880, to provide final proof of the claim. It is noteworthy that J.N. Bryan, a former enslaver of George Paysinger, is among these witness signatures.

The *Bossier Banner* published a notice on February 10, 1880, of the intention of George Paysinger to make final proof of his homestead claim on Tuesday, March 25, 1880. The publication listed the claim as no. 1039 for the eastern half of the southwest quarter and the western half of the southeast quarter of section 14, township 23, north of range 13, west of the Louisiana meridian. George completed the final affidavit required of homestead claimants at the Natchitoches, Louisiana Land Office on June 3, 1880.

The Natchitoches Land Office issued Final Certificate no. 434 for Homestead Application no. 1039 on August 3, 1882. This 160-acre homestead land patent was only a segment of the land George Paysinger acquired during his lifetime. Before the land patent was final, in 1877, the family that enslaved George before emancipation either deeded or sold him 140 acres. He also purchased another 160 acres from the Bossier Parish School Board in April 1885 and 40 acres of state land in 1887, totaling 500 acres. George lived out his life on the land he acquired, and a portion of the land remains with his heirs.

CONTRIBUTOR: *Felix Lewis Scott Jr. is the great-great-great-grandson of George Paysinger. Felix Scott Jr. is currently on a "retirement" exploration journey into his nuclear family and family history/genealogy, finding joy in unearthing extraordinary relations like his great-great-great-grandfather George Paysinger.*

MOSES SINGLETON

By Clara Robertson, Claretha Day and Caleb Ricard

Moses Singleton made his settlement in East Feliciana Parish, Louisiana, before 1870 and on the land he later acquired in 1901. Singleton completed Homestead Entry no. 21930 at the New Orleans, Louisiana Land Office, under the Homestead Act of 1862 and fulfilled all the requirements to receive patent no. 13009 on August 14, 1907. The 159.72 acres were located just east of East Feliciana Parish, Louisiana.

Moses was a sixty-seven-year-old farmer when he entered his final testimony for his land. During the years in which homesteaders were required to make proof in support of their entries, Moses Singleton, his wife, Priscilla Gray Singleton, and their five children made improvements to the property. They cleared and fenced about fifteen acres for six seasons and constructed a log house and a cotton house. Moses was the son of Melinda Verdun and the grandson of Mercelite Verdun, who were landowners in the Assumption Parish area, which gave him the incentive to follow their tradition.

Mercelite is listed in the 1860 census as an eighty-year-old free woman of color living in Assumption Parish, Louisiana. This would mean that she was born around 1780. The archives in Baton Rouge, Louisiana, give no listing of her birthdate, marriage or death. The land record shows that Mercelite lived on property located in Assumption Parish for five years, beginning in 1837, before making an application to buy the land at $1.25 per acre (135.7 acres). The agreement was completed in 1842 and witnessed by George Schwin. Mercelite stated that the land would be used to raise rice, potatoes and other foods to feed her children (Melinda, Daniel or Cade, Celestine and Matilda).

Melinda Verdine (Verdun) is listed in the 1860 census as a fifty-year-old woman of color living in Assumption Parish, Louisiana. This would mean that Melinda was born in the year 1810. Land records show that Melinda purchased 150 acres of government land, located in what is now Terrebonne, St. Mary and Assumption Parishes, in 1848. Melinda had one son who was born around 1840, Moses Singleton. He was fathered by an enslaved man named Cubic (Cubit) Singleton. There is no record of the place of birth, marriage or death of Melinda Verdine (Verdun), who resided in the St. Mary, Terrebonne or Assumption Parishes. Melinda and Cubic (Cubit) Singleton had six children, John, Hypolite, Moses, William, Elizabeth and Mary.

Several of Moses's neighbors and longtime acquaintances agreed to serve as the witnesses to testify for his homestead entry (Geo J. Reiley, Steve Bell, John Turner and William Williams) on December 26, 1906, to provide final proof for his claim. Steve Bell and John Turner completed the two witness testimonials.

The New Orleans Land Office published a notice on October 11, 1906, of the intention of Moses Singleton to make final proof of his homestead claim on October 10, 1900. The publication listed the claim for Homestead Entry no. 21930, for the northeast quarter of the southeast quarter, the south half of the southeast quarter and the southeast quarter of the southwest quarter of section 20 in township 3, south of range 3, east of the St. Helena meridian in Louisiana. Moses completed the final affidavit required of homestead claimants at the New Orleans, Louisiana Land Office on December 26, 1906. The New Orleans Land Office issued the final land certificate, no. 13009 on August 14, 1907.

Moses resided on the property until the time of his death. He and his wife reared five children, Louis Singleton Sr., James Singleton, Survice Singleton, Emma Singleton and Sarah Singleton.

CONTRIBUTORS: *Clara Robertson, Caleb Ricard and Claretha Day are the great-great-great-granddaughters of Moses Singleton, and Caleb Ricard is the grandson of Clara Robertson.*

CHARLES HENRY VEAL

By Alvin Blakes

Charles Henry Veal was born in December 1865 in St. Francisville, West Feliciana Parish, Louisiana. He married Clara McDaniel, who was born in 1875 in St. Francisville. They had four children, Mamie, Rose, Charles Jr. and Andrew.

Charles filed Homestead Application no. 11606 under the Homestead Act of 1862 in Baton Rouge, Louisiana. He submitted three applications before receiving approval for his land. The original application was filed on March 5, 1927; a second homestead entry was filed on December 9, 1927; and the final application was filed on January 26, 1929.

Charles made a final payment of $2.95 for the submission of the final application and signed his name for the grant for lots 1, 2 and 3, section

27, township 1S, range 4W, St. Helena meridian, Louisiana, containing 32.08 acres.

In the final affidavit, Charles, a native-born citizen of the United States, stated he made his actual settlement upon, cultivated and resided on the land from January 1, 1900, to January 26, 1929. Of the thirty-two acres, he cultivated twenty acres, and the remaining twelve acres yielded twelve thousand feet of saw timber. In 1924, his farm yielded twenty acres of cotton (two bales), corn (two hundred bushels), peas (sixty bushels) and potatoes (forty bushels).

He constructed his home in 1900 on the southeast corner of the land, and it contained a barn, an outhouse, wire fencing, hog pastures and pecan trees. The cost of materials was $1,000, and with $100 of nominal labor costs, the total value was $1,100.

Charles signed his final affidavit in West Feliciana Parish on December 10, 1929. There were two witnesses to his claim. James Peyton of Plettenberg, Louisiana, signed his affidavit in West Feliciana Parish on December 10, 1929. The other witness, Henry Williams of Solitude, Louisiana, departed from the state of Louisiana, and with his whereabouts unknown to either man, and since it was impossible to get a correction of his testimony as a proof witness for the claimant, his affidavit was signed by Charles Henry Veal and James Peyton.

Charles's proof of homestead claim notice was advertised in the *True Democrat*, a weekly newspaper printed in West Feliciana Parish, Louisiana. The United States Department of the Interior General Land Office issued Final Homestead Patent no. 1034646 on February 12, 1930.

CONTRIBUTOR: *Alvin Blakes is a descendant of the Veal family of Wilkinson County, Mississippi. Many of the early Veal family members were dispersed and taken to work in Pointe Coupee Parish, Rapides Parish and West Feliciana Parish in Louisiana, where Charles Henry Veal lived.*

ANDREW RICHARDSON AND SARAH JANE (FOSTER) RICHARDSON

By Dr. Antoinette Harrell

Andrew filed his homestead application, no. 2180, in the New Orleans Land Office on August 10, 1878. Andrew Richardson paid the sum of seven dollars for the entry of southwest quarter of the northeast quarter of section 34 in township 2, south of range 4, east St. Helena Parish, Louisiana, to the homestead receiver's office in New Orleans on March 7, 1871. The property containing 40.21 acres in section 34, township south of range 4E.

Two witnesses testified on behalf of the homestead claim: William H. Smith and Benjamin Pierce. They both stated they had known Sarah Richardson for eight years. They confirmed that Andrew "built an eighteen-by-twelve-foot-square house containing four rooms and lived in the house from the seventh day of March 1871, until his death." He made the following improvements to the land: he built a stable and shed, planted a vegetable garden, dug a water well and also planted a peach tree and other fruit trees.

According to the 1900 U.S. census, Andrew Richardson was born in St. Helena Parish, Louisiana, around 1852, and in the 1880 U.S. census, it was recorded that he was living in the Second Ward within the St. Helena Parish. His father was from Virginia, and his mother was from Georgia. His primary occupation was farming. Nathan and Dicy Harden Richardson were his parents. Among his siblings were Dan Richardson, Wesley Richardson and Mary Richardson.

Nathan and my great-great-great-great-grandmother Carrie were enslaved on the Benjamin and Celia Bankston Plantation in St. Helena Parish, Louisiana. Nathan and Carrie are believed to have been brother and sister through oral history accounts from the late Luella Vining Richardson. Nathan can be found in the inventory of Benjamin and Celia, dated May 30, 1855.

Andrew and his wife, Sarah Jane (Foster) Richardson, had seven children living with them when the 1900 U.S. census was taken (Alonzo, Monroe, Girtie, Clacie L., John H., Maraget and Leonard). He and Sarah were married for twenty-four years. Sarah Jane (Foster) Richardson was born on October 9, 1861. She died on July 9, 1912, and was buried in Black Greek AME Cemetery in St. Helena Parish, Louisiana, where Andrew was buried.

During the 1931 wedding of my maternal grandmother, Josephine Richardson Harrell, and my grandfather Jasper Leon Harrell Sr., Andrew's son John Wesley Richardson and his grandson Emmitt Nathaniel Richardson served as her witnesses. Emmitt and my grandmother were born only one year apart. The oral history and family connections of the Richardson family perished when many of the elderly members of the family passed away. This homestead entry provides evidence that Andrew Richardson and Thomas Richardson had a family connection.

CONTRIBUTOR: *Dr. Antoinette Harrell is a renowned genealogist and local historian with an emphasis in African American history in Tangipahoa & St. Helena, Louisiana Parishes. Dr. Harrell is committed to researching and documenting the untold stories of African Americans in the Louisiana Florida Parishes.*

GEORGE WILLIAMS AND CHESTER WILLIAMS

By Crystal Williams-Jackson

I remember reading something once that said, "From very early times, there have always been landowners or landholders." Numerous biblical accounts give us an idea of why land ownership was important. Abraham bargained with Ephron, the Hittite, for a burial place for his wife, Sarah. During a famine in Egypt, Joseph, a former slave, bought land for Pharaoh from Egyptian landowners in exchange for food. And Job, who lived in the land of Uz, owned property that he gave to his sons and daughters.[181]

George Williams, born enslaved around 1838, had a few things in common with the faithful men in these biblical accounts. The 1900 census shows George was a property owner and farmer who lived with his third wife, Lucy Moore. He planted and cultivated crops to sell and made it possible for one of his sons to become an entrepreneur and landowner. There is currently no information on how or when he began living in the Claiborne Parish, Louisiana area.

On October 14, 1907, George applied for the Adjoining Farm Homestead Entry no. 11177, 27.18 acres of land "for the benefit of his adjoining farm." He lived on the land with his third wife, Lucy, and his two youngest sons, Lem and Gordon (from his second wife, Frances Payne). His son Chester, along with his first wife, Icy (Banks), was the only adult child of the eleven who remained to work the land with his father. The older children had married and moved away to work and raise families in other areas and states.

The land entry papers say that George and his son Chester made improvements to the land as required. They added a wire fence, cleared eight acres and built the old log house. They cultivated about one and a

Chester Williams. *Courtesy of Crystal Williams-Jackson.*

half bales of cotton each year from 1908 to 1910. Sadly, George died around December 1910.

It was obvious that Chester knew the importance and significance of landownership, the powerful resource it was and the opportunities it would afford his descendants. He followed through with the acquisition of the adjoining farm homestead. He continued to work tirelessly, cultivating cotton, and he continued to live on the land with his second wife, Ada (Bishop), and his two children Chester Jr. and C.D. Williams.

In May 1913, the U.S. land office in Baton Rouge, Louisiana, received the final proof testimony of the claimant signed by twenty-four-year-old Chester Williams, the heir of George Williams. Included were testimony of witness documents from those who knew both George and Chester: Frank Waller, Charley Strochan, Ferrell Brown and Crawford Greer.

Frank Waller of Gordon, Louisiana, knew George for twenty-five years before his death and his son Chester for twenty years or more. He stated, "I lived right at the land and see them there every week and almost every day." According to the 1910 census, Frank and his two daughters Nora and Joanna lived right next door.

Charley Strochan (pronounced "strong") of Tubal, Arkansas, knew George for ten years and knew Chester as well. The 1910 census shows Charley and his family as being neighbors of Chester, his son Chester Jr., his older sister Nora and her children. By 1913, Charley and his family were living about a mile away from the land, and he stated that he saw them there each year; he passed by frequently and knew they cultivated the land. He thought the value of the improvements cost around $40.00 ($1,180.99 in 2022).

There were no testimony of witness statements or interviews included in the land entry documents for Charles "Ferrell" Brown or Crawford Greer, but both were found in the 1910 census, recorded as living near the land of George and Chester Williams. They were, as written by the clerk of Claiborne Parish, a couple of the "reputable white men by which he proposes to make his proof."

The heirs of George Williams received Homestead Land Patent no. 358820 on October 8, 1913, due to Chester Williams's commitment to continue to comply with the process to acquire the adjoining farmland.

Using Google Maps, I often find myself traveling virtually northeast on Highway 161 in Louisiana, and about a mile before I cross the state line into Arkansas, I glance to the right for a bird's-eye view of the land once owned by my family in Colquett, Claiborne Parish, Louisiana. We are unsure about when the land was sold or lost due to there being no oral family history passed down. I am grateful to have Chester's grandson and one of his nieces who grew up in Claiborne Parish as resources when I research our family history in that area. I look forward to finding out what became of the land and plan to see it in person one day along with other family members.

CONTRIBUTOR: *Crystal Williams-Jackson is the great-granddaughter of George Williams Sr. and the great-niece of Chester Williams Sr.*

HENRY AND JULIA GORDON

By Rex A. Holiday, PhD

Henry and Julia were enslaved by Dempsey Kemp Gorman, who acquired them along with their two-year-old daughter, Luisa, from his parents, David and Rebecca Gorman, on March 25, 1848.

Henry Gordon and Julia Gorman lived as a couple, but due to the laws of the day that prevented enslaved people from marrying, they were not married until several years after their emancipation, on March 29, 1869. A year and a half later, on November 18, 1870, Henry traveled to the Land Office of New Orleans to file a homestead application (no. 1824) for thirty-five acres under the Homestead Act, which was approved by the United States Congress on May 20, 1962. He paid seven dollars for the application fee and signed with an X because he had never learned to read or write.

Four years later, Henry and Julia, with the help of their children, had cultivated twenty-five of the thirty-five acres, building a kitchen, a corncrib and a stable. Unfortunately, on November 5, 1874, a little more than a year before the homestead agreement was to be finalized, Henry died, leaving behind his wife, Julia, and his ten children, Louisa, Elvira, Frank, Henry, Emelia, Sophia, Ike, Berlin, Nancy (also known as Sallie) and Harriet. This must have left Julia feeling a bit overwhelmed and uncertain about how she was going to pay the balance of the homestead agreement.

Left: Berlin Childress Gordon, the son of Henry and Julia Gordon. *Right*: Berlin Gordon, Hurley Gordon and Charlie Gordon are the son, grandson and great-grandson of Henry and Julia Gordon. *Courtesy of Dr. Rex Holiday.*

Despite this tremendously difficult time, Julia pressed forward and completed the homestead contract. With her former enslaver, Dempsey Kemp Gorman, signing as a witness, Julia paid the balance of ninety cents to become the rightful owner (according to Homestead Certificate no. 326 to application no. 1824 and Accession Serial no. LA0320_188) of 35.92 acres of the northeast quarter of the northeast fractional quarter of section 8 in township 3, south of range 5E on December 21, 1875. Due to the difficulty of traveling to the New Orleans land office, Julia was allowed to sign the final documents at the land office in Greensburg, St. Helena Parish.

Less than two years after signing the final documents for those 39.92 acres, Julia, along with her son Frank and her son-in-law Albert Jackson, sold 130 acres of land to Dempsey Kemp Gorman for the sum of $1,000 in July 1877.[182]

CONTRIBUTOR: *Dr. Holiday is a great-great-grandson of Henry and Julia Gordon's son Berlin. He is a part-time professor of intercultural communications for the University of Florida's College of Journalism and Communication Online.*

MOSES DYSON

By Jackie M.B. Chapman

Based on 1910 United States census data, Moses Dyson was the brother of my great-great-grandfather Isaac Dyson. In 1910, Clara Ann Dyson, the wife of Moses in prior census records, was living with Frederick and Sophia Dyson and was listed as a widow and "aunt" to Frederick, the head of household. Frederick Dyson was the son of Isaac and Elizabeth Dyson, my great-great-grandparents. In the 1870 and 1880 census records, it is recorded that Isaac had a son named Moses, who was the namesake of Isaac's brother.

According to data from the 1870, 1880 and 1900 United States census records, Moses was born in 1830 in Louisiana; his father was also born in Louisiana, and his mother was born in Tennessee. His wife, Clara Ann, was born in Louisiana between 1830 and 1840, according to 1870–1910 census data; she did not have any children per the 1900 census data. Clara Ann's parents were born in Virginia. Moses had two sisters and a niece residing with him and his wife in 1880—Matilda, single, fifty-two; and a younger sister, Esther Brumfield, a widow, forty; and Esther's daughter, Matilda Brumfield, seven. Moses died before the 1910 census, which was recorded on May 4. Clara Ann died after 1910. Their burial locations are unknown.

On April 3, 1872, Moses Dyson submitted Homestead Application no. 2874 to the land office in New Orleans, Louisiana. The tract of land consisted of 161.94 acres located in Washington Parish, Louisiana, near the Palestine Post Office. Moses paid the required application fees for the tract of land, which was legally described as the northeast quarter of the southeast quarter of section 29, the western half of the southwest quarter and the southeast quarter of the southwest quarter of section 28 in township 1, south of Range 9 east of the St Helena meridian.

At the age of forty-six, Moses settled on the land immediately and began building a home for himself and his wife. Over the next seven years, Moses built a kitchen and several out houses, and he cultivated and fenced about seventeen acres and planted crops of corn, cotton, potatoes and peas. With all the improvements, his homestead was valued at $150.

Moses's homestead proof claimant testimony, along with witness testimonies from his neighbors Daniel Dyson and Granville Tate, who confirmed the previously stated facts, was documented and certified on August 22, 1879, by Washington Parish judge James M. Burris. Moses and his witnesses signed the homestead documents with an X.

On September 9, 1879, Patent Certificate no. 1050 was issued for Homestead Application no. 2874. (Copies of original documents are held at National Archives and Records Administration in Washington, D.C.) However, the land office in New Orleans did not record the patent for almost three years. A potential legal issue was noted on the March 28, 1872 homestead affidavit, which Moses filed with the clerk of court in Washington Parish instead of the land office in New Orleans. Moses expressed in that affidavit that he had no means to travel to New Orleans to file the affidavit in which he swore that he satisfied all the requirements for a homestead. His claim was referred to the board of equitable adjudication on October 12, 1881, and confirmed and approved on December 2, 1881. After ten years, Moses Dyson's homestead patent was finally recorded on April 10, 1882, in vol. 2, page 493.

CONTRIBUTOR: *Jackie M.B. Chapman is the author of a blog, Coming Together with Isaac and Elizabeth Dyson. All of the nine offspring come together in one electronic file and bring generations of their descendants together at a MEGA DYSON Tailgate, where some four hundred family members attended.*

MOSES BRUMFIELD

By Lyle Gibson

In January 1875, Moses Brumfield settled on his land located in Tangipahoa Parish, Louisiana. He submitted Homestead Application no. 4101 on December 26, 1874, for 160 acres of land located on section 20, the northern half of the southwest quarter and the eastern half of the southeast quarter of section 19 in township 1, south of range 8E.

Per the homestead application, Moses signed with an X. His final proof testimony stated that he had no family. He also stated that he had lived on the land since January 1875 and cleared twenty acres for cultivation, which was fenced. He raised corn, cotton, oats and sweet potatoes. His dwellings included a house, a smokehouse, a barn stable and other outhouses. The value of his improvements totaled $500. His witnesses were Fred Brumfield of Osyka, Pike County, Mississippi; H.W.L. Lewis of Osyka, Pike County, Mississippi; and Judge Dean. Both Snipes and Dean concurred in their statements regarding the twenty acres of improved land and the presence of a dwelling house, a smokehouse, a barn stable and other outhouses. His original home was burned and rebuilt in September 1879. Moses received Homestead Patent no. 1263 on June 30, 1882, for 160 acres.

According to primary source documentation, Moses Brumfield was born in March 1837 in Louisiana. In the 1870 Tangipahoa Parish, Louisiana census, he is enumerated with a twelve-year-old girl named Anna Brumfield and a fifteen-year-old boy name Nelson Alford.[183] In the 1880 Tangipahoa Parish, Louisiana Census, Moses, forty-seven, is the only person listed in the household.[184] In the 1900 Tangipahoa Parish, Louisiana census, Moses, seventy-three, is enumerated with his wife, Roda, born in January 1860; son Obediah, born in October 1882; daughter Losa, born in December 1888; daughter Idella, born in February 1892; and daughter Sena, born in June 1893.[185] This 1900 census also lists Moses as having been married twice and Roda giving birth to three children, all of whom were still living at the time of the census. One could infer that Obediah was born during the first marriage of Moses. Additionally, the Louisiana Deaths 1850–1875, 1894–1960 database lists that Cerrey Dyson died on June 19, 1917, in Tangipahoa, Louisiana. Her parents were listed as Mose Brumfield and Rodie Brumfield (certificate no. 6415, record no. 121).[186]

CONTRIBUTOR: *Lyle Gibson is a genealogist with thirty-one years of experience and a historian with over twenty years of teaching experience. Gibson authored a book about a multiracial American family from the colonial period to the early twentieth century titled* Black Tie White Tie.

LABRON BROCK

By Dr. Antoinette Harrell

Twenty-six-year-old Labron Brock filed his homestead application, no. 8305, with the New Orleans Land Office on September 22, 1884. According to the 1880 United States census, Labron (Laben) was living with his father, Andrew Brock; stepmother, Julia Anne (Bankston) Brock; and his siblings, Julia, Louis, Nathaniel, Rachel and Oscar). Also in the household were his stepmother's siblings, Jane and Bailey Bankston.

Before settling on the land in Louisiana, Labron indicated in his application that he lived with William Brock (the possible enslaver of his family) in Mississippi. William Brock also acquired homesteaded land and may have encouraged Labron to apply for his land.

Labron noted the following improvements to his land in 1884. He built a house valued at $30, a smokehouse valued at $12 and a stable and crib worth $20. His garden was valued at $10. About twenty acres of land were cleared and fenced, worth approximately $80. He built a sixteen-by-sixteen-foot house constructed of pine logs and lumber with two doors, a chimney and a gallery covered by pine boards. Upon its completion on January 1, 1885, the house was occupied. During his first few years on the property, Labron planted six acres of crops. Each year, he added more acres until twenty acres were cultivated. Cotton, corn and potatoes were raised on the farm, valued at $150. His farm animals included one horse, two oxen, two cattle, twelve hogs and twenty-four chickens.

Labron married Elizabeth Conerly on January 16, 1887, and he made it clear that his "family lived with him all of the time" since submitting his claim. A notice was published in the *Franklin New Area* newspaper beginning on November 27, 1889, for six consecutive weeks to announce that Labron would submit his final claim for the homesteaded land. Several witnesses from Washington Parish were ready to testify on his behalf, including Josiah Brumfield, Willis Brumfield, Jordan Lee and Green Andrews. Willis Brumfield and Jordan Lee did provide actual written testimony attesting to Labron's continuous residence and cultivation of the land.

He submitted his final affidavit required for the homestead claimant by signing X on December 4, 1889. After satisfying all of the requirements, Labron Brock successfully obtained Homestead Patent Certificate no. 3926 for 82.93 acres of land in Washington Parish, Louisiana, on June 25, 1892.

In the 1900 U.S. census, Labron was listed as a thirty-nine-year-old farmer, and it stated that had been married for thirteen years. The couple's children were Corene, Lula, Sylvia, Minnie, Julia, Rachel and Caroline. Elizabeth Brock passed away on April 29, 1921, and Labron continued to live on the land well into the 1930s.

Labron impressed me a great deal, because he applied for this land at a young age (twenty-six) and demonstrated his determination to comply with every step required of him to become a landowner. His great-granddaughter Pasty Zanders Johnson is so proud of her paternal great grandfather. Patsy's father, Labron, is the grandson of Labron through his mother's lineage.

CONTRIBUTOR: *Dr. Antoinette Harrell is a renowned genealogist and local historian with an emphasis in African American history in Tangipahoa and St. Helena Parishes, Louisiana.*

JOSIAH CYPRIAN

By Bernice A. Bennett

Josiah Cyprian was born around 1840, enslaved on the Henry Cooper Plantation on the Tchefuncte River, about fifteen miles from Madisonville in St. Tammany Parish, Louisiana.

Around the age of eighteen or twenty, Josiah Cyprian enlisted on August 17, 1864, in Company G, Tenth Regiment of United States Colored Heavy Artillery Volunteers at the Touro building in New Orleans. He was discharged on February 22, 1867. He married his first wife, Arina (Rena M. Linton), in 1868, and they later divorced on July 9, 1892, in the district court for St. Tammany Parish in Covington, Louisiana.[187]

Cyprian applied for an invalid pension, no. 971991, on October 18, 1890, and resided in St. Tammany Parish. He married his second wife, Alice Cecelia Lotten, on November 6, 1895, in the presence of the following witnesses: Reverend Joshua Penn, Joseph Cuprier, George Richardson and Alice Brown. Alice was born in North Carolina in 1838 and was a midwife in Louisiana. Cyprian was a farmer.

Despite Josiah Cyprian's disabilities, at the age of sixty, he submitted Homestead Application no. 18603 at the New Orleans Land Office on October 28, 1897, for 40.44 acres. This land is located at the southwest quarter of the northeast quarter of section 8, township 5, south of range 10E, St. Helena meridian. He could read and write, and his signature can be seen on the application.

The land was ordinary pine land, suitable for farming. The actual residence was inhabited on November 18, 1897, and Cyprian cleared eighteen acres. His improvements also included the construction of a log dwelling house, a barn and a stable, all valued at $300.

In addition, Cyprian's household included his wife and ten children. The children's names and birthdates were recorded in the invalid pension record: Laura, September 2, 1866; Joseph, August 20, 1868; Emma, September 22, 1870; John, May 26, 1872; Mathew, February 23, 1872; Martha, March 13, 1877; Luke, October 15, 1881; Mark, December 20, 1883; Joshua, January 20, 1885; and Sarah, September 19, 1887.

The *St. Tammany Farmer* was a weekly newspaper, and it listed the following witnesses who were to testify on behalf of Josiah: B. Neil, Emile Baham, Robert Brown and Tom Cyprian from Verger, Louisiana. This notice was certified by register Walter L. Cohen. Forty-two-year-old B. Neil and thirty-year-old Emile Baham corroborated Josiah's testimony about the length of time he lived on the land and the improvements he made.

Josiah Cyprian received his homestead land patent certificate, no. 11840, on December 21, 1904. Upon the death of Josiah in 1923, Alice Cyprian filed for the widow's pension, no. WC 1205391, on May 14, 1923. She had two children; the other children were from Josiah's first wife, Rena. Five of those children were still alive during her many discussions with the pension board to obtain the money she needed to survive at her old age. Alice died in August 1928 in Folsom, Louisiana.

CONTRIBUTOR: *Bernice Alexander Bennett is an award-winning author, genealogist, nationally recognized guest speaker, storyteller and producer-host of the popular Research at the National Archives and Beyond BlogTalkRadio program.*

JOHN TURNER

By Clara Robertson, Claretha Day and Caleb Ricard

According to the 1880 U.S. census, John Turner was born around 1871 to Duncan and Julia Turner in St. Helena Parish, Louisiana; they had six children in total. Duncan and Julia Turner were born in Mississippi.[188]

John Turner made his settlement in St. Helena Parish, Louisiana, on July 1, 1900, before later acquiring the land in 1905. Turner completed Homestead Entry no. 21150 at the New Orleans, Louisiana Land Office under the Homestead Act of 1862 and fulfilled the requirements to receive patent no. 12327 on November 8, 1905. The 159.74 acres were located just south of East Feliciana Parish, Louisiana.[189]

John was thirty-six years old when he entered his final testimony for his land. During the years in which homesteaders were required to make proof in support of their entries, John Turner; his wife, Phoebe (Stevenson) Turner; their nine children; and John's younger brother Charles made improvements to the property. They had a log dwelling, a corn crib, stables, a hay house and a cotton house for a total cost of about $450.

On March 22, 1905, several of John's neighbors and close friends agreed to serve as witnesses to testify for his final proof of his homestead entry claim: Stephen Bell, John Turner, William Williams, George J. Reiley and Moses Singleton. Stephen Bell and Moses Singleton (also a homesteader) completed the two witness testimonials.

The New Orleans Land Office published a notice on March 25, 1905, of intention of John Turner to make final proof of his homestead claim in 1900. The publication listed the claim for Homestead Entry no. 21150, for the east quarter of the southeast quarter of section 19 and the west quarter of the southwest quarter of section 20 in township 3 south of range 3E of St. Helena meridian, Louisiana. The land was patented on November 8, 1905, after having been approved on September 29, 1905, at the New Orleans Land Office, with Final Certificate no. 12327.[190]

John Turner had two minor issues with his application. The first was a clerical issue with his advertisement. It was not published or had issues being published. He was also short $3.50. Once this was amended, his application was submitted for review and approval.

Contributors: *Clara Robertson, Caleb Ricard and Claretha Day are the great-great-great-granddaughters of Moses Singleton, and Caleb Ricard is the grandson of Clara Robertson.*

LEANDER YOUNGBLOOD

By Bernice A. Bennett

Leander Youngblood filed his homestead application, no. 11610 on September 28, 1887, to settle on public land with his wife, Lucy J. (Bromfield) Youngblood. By December 1888, Leander had made improvements to this land located on lots 1, 2, 3 and 4 of section 31, township 1S, range 10E of the St. Helena meridian containing 127.20 acres of land.

In the 1880 U.S. census, it was recorded that Leander and his wife, Lucy, resided in Edward Dykes, Washington Parish, Louisiana, with their two children, Ella Youngblood and Alonzo L. Youngblood. By the time Leander applied for his homestead, he had five additional children, Vesti, Rosa Jane, Anderson, Lettie and Josephine.

In compliance with requirements under the Homestead Act, Leander Youngblood made improvements to his land by adding a dwelling house, a kitchen, a smokehouse, a crib, stables, an outhouse and a garden, with a total value of $500. He noted in his land entry testimony that his wife and their seven children had lived on the land continuously since they had first settled on the property. Leander initially cleared fifteen acres, and after six seasons, he was able to raise 45 acres of crops. The land was described as ordinary farming land, most valuable for agriculture.

Several individuals were listed as witnesses on his land entry papers and also in the *Franklinton New Era* newspaper on October 17, 1894. His witnesses were Thomas Green, Green James, Isaac Fortenberry and Clinton Harvey. Both Thomas Green and Isaac Fortenberry of Mount Point, Louisiana, verified that Leander had complied with the homesteading rules and supported his claimant testimony. Isaac Fortenberry and Clinton Harvey had also applied for a homestead in Washington Parish.

Leander Youngblood submitted his final affidavit required for the homestead claimant by signing X on December 4, 1894. Upon satisfying all of the requirements, Leander Youngblood successfully obtained Land Patent no. 5791 on January 25, 1896, for 127.20 acres of land in Washington Parish, Louisiana.

While Leander Youngblood and his wife, Lucy, do not appear in the 1900 census, six of their children lived together. Their oldest son, Alonzo Youngblood, was listed as the head of the household, with Vesti, Rosa Jane, Anderson, Letti and Josephine all living together. Alonzo was enumerated as a farmer who owned the land he lived and worked on.

CONTRIBUTOR: *Bernice Bennett is the great-great-granddaughter of Peter Clark and Rebecca Youngblood Clark and the great-great-great granddaughter of Thomas and Minerva Youngblood. She is currently exploring how Leander maybe related to her Youngblood family.*

5

MISSISSIPPI BLACK
HOMESTEADERS

*I am true to my own race. I wish to see all done that can be done for their
encouragement, to assist them in acquiring property, in becoming intelligent,
enlightened, useful, valuable citizens.*
—Hiram Rhodes Revels, first Black senator from Mississippi (1869–71)

Through the 1862 Homestead Act, many Black Americans in Mississippi
owned land. The stories highlighted in this chapter are from Amite,
Woodville, Choctaw, Franklin, Lauderdale and Simpson Counties.
The diversity of these locations demonstrates the level of support in these
communities to apply for and complete the homestead application process.
According to the Homestead National Historical Park Service's research,
24,126 homesteaders were awarded land in Mississippi. The total acreage
of homesteaded land was 2,637,412, representing 9 percent of the land in
the state. These homesteaders' descendants are proud to share how their
ancestors successfully obtained land in Mississippi.

IRVIN BRUMFIELD

By Nona Edwards-Thomas, MD

Ervin (Irvin) Brumfield was born in 1846 in Mississippi. Irvin, along with
his parents, Liddie Brumfield Caston (1825–1916, Mississippi) and Louis
Brumfield (birth and death dates are unknown), was enslaved in Mississippi.

No information concerning what happened to Louis Brumfield is known at this time. Liddie and Louis Brumfield had four sons, Irvin and his three brothers, Tom, Richard and Frank Brumfield. They were identified as siblings through interviewing their descendants and family members and DNA analysis. Upon the death of her husband, Liddie Brumfield married Calvin Caston.

At the age of twenty-four, Brumfield filed homestead application no. 4290 on September 1, 1870, for eighty acres of land in Pike County, Mississippi, at the land office in Jackson, Hinds County, Mississippi, for a fee of seven dollars. [191]

Irvin and Louisa Brumfield were married in 1873. During the seven years on the homestead settlement, he made improvements to the land by cultivating thirty acres and building a house, a corn crib and stables. There is no value of improvements stated on the homestead application.

On the final proof document dated August 21, 1877, Henry Conerly and Calvin Caston (Irvin Brumfield's stepfather) are listed as his witnesses. They

Irvin Brumfield's tombstone. *Courtesy of Nona L. Edwards-Thomas.*

verified that Irvin Brumfield (name listed as Ervine Brumfield) was on the land beginning on September 1, 1870, and during that time, he was the head of a family consisting of a wife and four children. However, later documentation supports the fact that Irvin's wife was Louisa McEwen Brumfield and they had a total of ten children (Martha Ann, Sherman, William, Irvin Jr., Louis, George, Isom, Daisy, Mamie and Mattie).[192]

The four eldest children were not listed on the application. However, Irvin's children, at that time, were Martha Ann, Sherman, Irvin Jr. and William.

On August 30, 1877, he submitted a balance fee of two dollars for the homestead and satisfied the requirements for the homestead patent.

On the patent, Irvin's name is recorded as Ervine Brumfield. However, for some unknown reason, Irvin Brumfield was enumerated in the 1880 U.S. census as Louis Brumfield. He resided with his wife, Louisa, and their five children, Martha Ann, Sherman, Irvin Jr., William and Louis. In the Pike County, Mississippi 1881 tax roll and the 1900 U.S. census, he is also enumerated as Irvin Brumfield. [193]

He received his homestead certificate, no. 938, on June 30, 1881. In the 1881 personal property tax roll, he owned two horses and two carriages valued at sixty and forty dollars, respectively.

He lived on the settlement with his family until his death in 1900. He was buried in the Caston Cemetery, an old cemetery about fifty feet off the road at 4022 Old 24 Extension Road, Magnolia, Mississippi.

CONTRIBUTOR: *Nona L. Edwards-Thomas, MD, is the great-granddaughter of Irvin Brumfield. Since 2012, Nona has run a blog titled* Brumfield Genealogy and Other Branches and Trees.

EUROPE BATES

By Dr. Antoinette Harrell

Europe Bates was born enslaved in Amite County, Mississippi, around 1834. Both of his parents were also born in Mississippi. Europe was married twice; his first wife was Violy (Vicie) Allen.

According to the 1870 and 1880 United States Censuses, Europe and Vicie were the parents of Sallie, Ellen, Susan and Howell Bates. After the death of Vicie in 1893, Europe married Eliza Jackson Bates in 1894. According

Howard Bates, the son of Europe Bates. *Courtesy of the Bates family.*

to the 1900 United States census, Europe and Eliza were still living in Beat 5, Amite, Mississippi, with Eliza's children and two of Europe's grandchildren. Europe owned his home and farm. He died in 1910 in Amite County, Mississippi, and was buried in the Bates Cemetery there.

Europe Bates submitted his application, no. 3582, at the land office in Jackson, Mississippi on November 19, 1869, for 165.64 acres of land. This entry was submitted under the provision of the act of Congress approved in 1866 for "Homestead Settlements in the States of Mississippi, Louisiana, Alabama, Arkansas and Florida." Europe signed his X, solemnly swearing that he was the head of his family, over the age of twenty-one and a citizen of the United States.

Abraham Taylor and Adam Harness were witnesses to Bates's homestead claim and attested that they had known Europe Bates for fifteen years (Adam Harness and his brother Esau were also homesteaders in the area). After meeting all the requirements to prove up, Europe submitted his final proof on October 2, 1876. He cleared fifty-five acres of the total 165.42 acres. His improvements included one dwelling, one corncrib, a cotton house, a shop, a kitchen and two small cabins. He was issued patent no. 937 for 165.64 acres of land on September 15, 1883, in Amite County, Mississippi.

In 1887 and 1888, Europe Bates was appointed as an inspector, overseeing elections for two years for the Tickfaw Precinct. The Europe Bates School for African American Children opened its doors in the late 1800s and was named after Europe Bates. His family donated the land for the school. The Bateses were a prominent family in Amite County, and the school later became a Rosenwald School. Much of the land that belonged to the Bates family in Amite County, Mississippi, remains in their possession today.

CONTRIBUTOR: *Dr. Antoinette Harrell is the great-great-great-granddaughter of Rebecca Ann Bates of Amite County, Mississippi.*

SAMUEL BROWN

By Sandra Williams Bush

Samuel Brown was born in April 1864 in Amite County, Mississippi. The 1880 U.S. census of beat 3, Simpson County, Mississippi, recorded that his parents were Willis and Amy Brown. Samuel, fourteen, had six siblings in 1880, Charles, eighteen; Benjamin, sixteen; Lucy, eleven; Merta, nine; George, five; and Orlena, eight months.

Sam Brown and Mary Stamps of Rankin County, Mississippi, were married on April 10, 1885, in Simpson County, Mississippi.[194] In 1887, after two years of marriage, Sam and Mary, along with their baby daughter, Luella, established an actual residence on land in Westville, Simpson County, Mississippi.

Brown could neither read nor write. On January 2, 1890, he placed his mark on the final affidavit required of homestead claimants, swearing to the fact that he was a native-born American citizen, born in Mississippi, and the head of his family. He paid a fee of seven dollars.[195]

Homestead proof testimony was provided by Brown and two witnesses: Jim Steel and King Thompson. On January 16, 1897, they all attested to the fact that Samuel Brown and his family had continually lived on the land and that the building improvements were valued at seventy-five dollars. Additionally, Brown and his witnesses affirmed that Samuel had farmed fifteen acres over ten seasons. In his years living on the land, Brown established his claim by building a sixteen-by-twenty-foot home, a crib (for crops), a stable and an outhouse. Brown and his wife had farmed the land and raised their children there for ten years before receiving the U.S. land grant.

On March 19, 1897, at the age of thirty-three, Brown made a final payment of two dollars to the Land Office of Jackson, Mississippi for the 79.66 acres of land he had settled on in Simpson County, Mississippi. He was issued a land patent on June 7, 1897.[196]

The 1900 U.S. census of beat 3, Simpson, Mississippi, lists Samuel Brown as a farmer and the owner of his land. Brown's family included his wife, Mary, and their children, Luella, Ida, Fannie, Whit, Simon, Willie, Sam and an infant son. Mary and her husband had two additional children, Noah, born in 1902, and Elizabeth, born in 1905.

Samuel Brown died in 1909. In the 1910 U.S. census of beat 3, Simpson County, Mississippi, Mary Brown is listed as a widow and the owner of the family farm.

By the 1920 U.S. census it is recorded that Mary Stamps Brown had moved to Cuyahoga County, Ohio, with her four youngest children, William, twenty-three; Samuel Jr., twenty-one; Noah, nineteen; and Elizabeth, fourteen.[197]

CONTRIBUTOR: *Sandra Williams Bush is the great-granddaughter of Samuel Brown. She is a retired librarian and has been working on collecting her family's history for twenty years.*

PRINCE DUNBAR

By the Gordon Williams Family and Denise Griggs

Prince Dunbar was born in February 1875 in Amite County, Mississippi. His mother was Rachel Dunbar, who was born in 1850. His siblings were Burk Henderson, Alfred, Jacob and Lorely Dunbar.[198]

Prince married Ione Pickett (1875–1917), the daughter of Richard "Jake" Pickett and Harriet Harrell, on January 18, 1897.[199] Ione's grandparents were Josh Harrell and America Hunt-Harrell/Harrold. Ione's grandmother America and her uncle Peter Hunt were both homesteaders before Prince filed a homestead application.

Prince and Ione had three daughters, Maggie, Janie and Alice Dunbar, when he filed for his homestead claim for 116.20 acres of land in White Apple, Mississippi, on January 18, 1901. His application was no. 36420, and he and his family settled on the land in February 1901, which comprised both timber and farming land. However, his land claim was suspended in

The great-great-grandchildren of Prince Dunbar. *Courtesy of the Gordon Williams family.*

1903 over a name error with one of Prince's witnesses, Josh Starks. Prince had to prove that Josh Starks was, in fact, the same man as Joshua Starks.

On April 21, 1906, Prince gave notice of publication at the Franklin County Chancery Clerk's Office in Meadville, Mississippi, to publish his intent for improving the property for a total of five weeks. His witnesses were his neighbors: Obb (Obrey) Morgan, Josh (Joshua) Starks, Lim (Lem) Wade and Howard Weeks. The witnesses verified that Prince Dunbar built a dwelling place, a kitchen, a smokehouse and a corn crib made of logs, which were valued at $200. The final proof for Prince Dunbar's homestead was given on July 2, 1906, and Prince was awarded his land patent on October 24, 1906. Three of his witnesses, Josh, Lim and the son of Howard Weeks married into the family of Richard and Harriet Pickett, who were the parents of Ione. Ione died in 1917, and Prince died on February 18, 1918.

CONTRIBUTORS: *Gordon "Kaakska Kweenow" Williams is the great-great-grandson of Prince Dunbar and Ione Pickett Dunbar through their daughter Janie Dunbar-Whitehead (Zeb). His great-great-great-grandmother America Harrold was also a homesteader.*

DANER GIBSON

By Denise I. Griggs

Daner Gibson was born on April 6, 1874, in Knoxville, Franklin County, Mississippi. His parents were Payne Gibson and Amanda Oats.[200]

Daner paid a fee of $6.77 on May 1, 1901, and by July 1901, he had completed the construction of his house. He and his new wife, Indiana "Indy," moved to the property on August 3, 1901. The land was composed of timber and was good for agricultural purposes. Afterward, Daner improved his property by building a dwelling place, a kitchen, a corncrib and a cotton house (all made with lumber). He farmed up to fifteen acres over five seasons. The total value of the land and dwellings was $200.

Daner listed his witness as Charley Edwards, William "Bill" Miller, Wilbur Ewell and Berg Fleming, but only Daner himself, Charley Edwards and William Miller were the final witnesses. They listed their nearest post office as Knoxville, Mississippi.

Daner was advised on September 1, 1904, that if he chose to prove his claim through another agent, according to the law of January 1904, it would delay his patent. Daner chose to keep the chancery clerk in Meadville and advised them on September 4, 1904. He next placed his notice of publication for his patent in Meadville, Mississippi, on September 29, 1906. His proof of publication was posted weekly in Meadville, Mississippi, from October 4, 1906, to November 1, 1906. His certificate as to final posting was listed in the *Searchlight* newspaper on November 12, 1906.

Daner's application was approved April 19, 1907, for the southern half of the northwest quarter of section 49, township 5N, range 1E. His first fee for the property was paid on May 31, 1901, in the amount of $7.00. The final fee of $1.77 was paid on November 12, 1906. Daner received his land patent, no. 19908, the following year. Daner, his wife and four children, Luther, Cornelius (Bully), Fannie and Payne, were living on the land. By 1931, Daner and Indiana had nine more children, Willie, Done, Thad, Albert (Bob), Sarah, Etta, Dick, L.C. and Thelma Ruth. Daner died on March 30, 1938.[201]

CONTRIBUTOR: *Daner Gibson's mother, Amanda Oats, was the sister-in-law of Denise's great-great-aunt Jane Harrell-Oats. Jane was the daughter of Denise's great-great-great-grandmother America Hunt-Harrell. Jane was also the sister of Denise's great-great-grandmother Margaret Hunt.*

AMERICA HUNT HARRELL/HAROLD

By Denise I. Griggs

America Hunt, a mixed-race woman, was born into slavery in Kentucky in approximately 1820. By 1840, Henry Hunt was her enslaver, and she lived on his plantation near Liberty, Amite County, Mississippi. America had children by Henry Hunt (proven through DNA). Two of the children were Margaret and Peter Hunt.[202] Oral family history states that Margaret was a weaver on the plantation and that Peter was a tanner of animal hides. America also had children by another enslaved man named Joshua/Josh Hunt, and they had five daughters born to them after America gave birth to children by Henry Hunt.

In approximately 1856, Henry Hunt moved his family and enslaved people from Amite County to Franklin County, Mississippi, near Roxie. Emancipation occurred on January 1, 1863; yet in 1865, Josh, America, their children and other formerly enslaved people were still farming on Henry Hunt's property. They were enumerated in the "Registry of

An image of Denise, Oscar Pickett and Delores Griggs. *Courtesy of Denise Griggs.*

Freedmen" as residing on the plantation of Henry Hunt in Franklin County, Mississippi.[203]

In 1870, their former enslaver, Henry Hunt, died, and Joshua and America changed their name from Hunt to Harrell, along with their daughters, Jane Harrell-Oats (John), Harriet Harrell-Pickett (Richard "Jake"), Louisa Harrell-Jackson (Winston), Mary Harrell-Starks (Levington) and Sarah Harrell.[204]

By February 1883, America was a widow when she filed for a 39.35-acre homestead application, no. 14748. Within nine years, America, with the help of her children, other relatives and hired hands, built a sixteen-by-sixteen-foot-square log cabin, which consisted of a bed, a bureau, chairs and a table. They also built three log corncribs. America farmed fifteen acres of the land, planting corn and potatoes, as the rest of the land comprised piney woods.

The neighbors who were witnesses for her final homestead application were J.M. Halford, "G.C." George Columbus Adams and Joe Turner. The two closest people living next to America were her neighbors Ben Lands and her son Peter Hunt, who, before his mother, also homesteaded 157.38 acres next to America's property. When America proved up on her homestead, her farm yielded one hundred bushels of corn and fifty bushels of potatoes. She owned plows, hoes, a turning plow, a weeder, one horse, five head of cattle and one yearling. In 1892, America's land, home and corn cribs were valued at $130. America was seventy-two years old.

Although America began life as an enslaved person, after twenty years of freedom, she was able to acquire land, live in her own home, work for herself and never be enslaved to anyone again. In approximately 1895, America died in Franklin County, Mississippi.

CONTRIBUTOR: *Denise I. Griggs and her identical twin sister, Delores, are the great-great-great-granddaughters of America Hunt Harrell. Denise is an award-winning author and founder of Blue Eclipse Publishing and Glass Tree Books.*

PETER HUNT

By Denise I. Griggs and Hunt Descendants

Peter Hunt was born enslaved on August 5, 1844, in Amite County, Mississippi, on the plantation of Henry Hunt. Hunt's mixed-race mother, America, was enslaved, and his father, Henry Hunt, was her enslaver.[205] According to the family's history, Peter was trained to be a tanner on the plantation. In approximately 1856, Henry Hunt moved his family and enslaved people from Amite County to Franklin County, Mississippi.[206]

In January 1864, exactly one year after being emancipated from slavery, Peter enlisted in the Union army's newly formed United States Colored Troops (USCT), Sixth Heavy Artillery, Company L, serving until 1866.[207] Peter was described in his pension papers as a mixed-race man; five feet, ten inches tall; with gray eyes; and hard to distinguish from a white man.[208]

One month after enlisting in the USCT, Peter caught the measles and was in the regimental hospital for one month, where he almost died. Although he remained in the USCT for two more years, he became partially disabled from his bout with the measles.

In 1872, Peter married Emily Shavers, and in 1873, their only child, Albert Hunt, was born. In 1874, Peter filed a homestead application for 157.38 acres of land based on the May 1862 Homestead Act. Due to his disability, friends and family helped Peter work the land. He built a home, cultivated 25.00 acres for farming and

Peter Hunt. *Courtesy of Denise Griggs.*

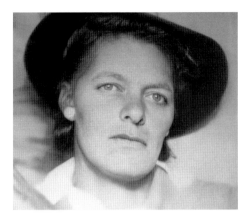 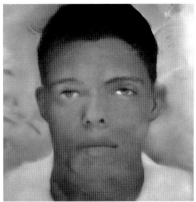

Left: Pearla Hunt, the granddaughter of Peter Hunt. *Right*: Albert Hunt, the great-grandson of Peter Hunt. *Courtesy of the Hunt family.*

built five structures on it: two corncribs, one kitchen, one smokehouse and one cotton house. His witnesses were Richard "Jake" Pickett and Nat Foster. Although Peter had been taught how to read and write, he signed his homestead papers with an X. He received his land patent, no. 1131, on August 3, 1881.

In 1886, Peter's sister Margaret died, and Peter and his wife, Emily, took in and raised Margaret's three children: Abel, Eula and Abigail. In 1892, Peter's mother, America Harrell/Harrold, also obtained a homestead on an adjourning 39.35 acres of land and received her land patent. In approximately 1895, America died a free woman and a landowner.

In September 1887, Peter filed for his military pension, which began an arduous series of events for him.[209] Initially, he was denied, but it was discovered that the military had his records combined with those of another soldier named Peter Hunt. His case was proven by vastly differing physical descriptions and the different names of the mothers of these men. Witnesses sent letters or appeared in person to verify and vouch for his health before Peter enlisted in the military, and his lifelong disabilities. One witness was Peter's white half-brother, a former Confederate soldier, who, in January 1907, gave testimony on Peter's behalf.[210] Afterward, Peter's pension rose from six dollars per month to twelve dollars.

On March 7, 1907, Peter's wife, Emily Shavers, died. Their only child, Albert, and his wife, Arlone, had eight of their ten children when Emily died: John, Charley, Houston, Wilson, Thompson, Margaret, Cornelious and Claricy. Another daughter, Pearla, was born in 1909, a few years before

Peter died, and one more daughter, Virginia, was born in 1919, after Peter died. Peter died on June 7, 1915, in Franklin County, Mississippi.[211]

As a former USCT soldier, Peter is listed on the African American Civil War Memorial in Washington, D.C., plaque no. A-16.[212]

CONTRIBUTORS: *Franklin, Bill, Marilyn, John, Michael, Albert and Deborah Hunt are the great-great-grandchildren of Peter Hunt. Michael Wright, is the great-great-great-grandson of Peter Hunt. Denise I. Griggs is the great-great-great-great-grandniece of Peter Hunt and is one of her family's genealogists, with almost forty years of experience.*

JACOB RAMSEY

By Jonnie Ramsey Brown

By the time I became fascinated with my family history, it was too late for any living person to give me a firsthand account of the lives of my paternal great-grandparents Jacob and Leanna Ramsey. However, my father was able to share some oral history about his grandfather Jacob, including the fact that Jacob owned land in Toomsuba, Lauderdale County, Mississippi, about twelve miles east of Meridian.

"The Old Place" was the term of endearment given to the land where Jacob and Leanna resided, and that location remained the anchor of the family, even after the home burned to the ground and long after Jacob and Leanna had passed on. One of my father's earliest recollections was his fifth birthday celebration at the "Old Place" in 1920. Many of his relatives lived nearby and came to celebrate with Daddy. There was plenty of food, including freshly fried chicken and home-baked pies and cakes. Daddy fondly remembered his early years on the family land, inspiring me to learn more.

When researching the land in the late 1990s, I discovered that a land patent had been issued to Jacob Ramsey on October 1, 1901. Several years after my discovery, I requested the case files from the National Archives in Washington, D.C., having learned of the existence of these documents and that they are a treasure-trove of historical and genealogical information.[213] When the envelope arrived, I was so excited, anticipating that an incredible story was about to unfold about my great-grandfather.

Jacob, like most Black Americans after the Civil War, knew that property ownership was the key to independence, financial stability, control over their own lives and respect. In 1884, Jacob applied at the Jackson, Mississippi Land Office, for application no. 23110, and acquired 80.02 acres—the southern half of the southeast quarter of section 19, township 7N, range 18E of the Choctaw principal meridian.

Jacob accomplished all the designated steps to acquire land but not without several setbacks and challenges. He misplaced the receipt given to him at the time of his claim, and he did not prove his claim within the five-year period required by law. Jacob filed several forms throughout the years relating to his claim, but for many reasons, the process was not satisfactorily completed to obtain final title to the land for seventeen years.

On November 28, 1890, Jacob filed for an additional homestead affidavit on the same land—six years after the original claim of 1884. On February 24, 1891, Jacob again filed for another homestead on the same land—seven years after the original claim of 1884. Was Jacob attempting to restart the proof process since the five years to prove up had been exceeded? On November 22, 1892, Jacob filed an affidavit summarizing the improvements made on the land—a dwelling house and outhouse, and he was farming between thirty-five and forty acres of improved land.

On February 24, 1899, a date again beyond the new five-year proof period, Jacob paid a $7.00 fee to settle the land temporarily. On June 25, 1900, Jacob paid $4.25 to post notice of his claim in the *Meridian Daily News*; the claim was also posted in the land office.

The homestead proof, testimony of claimant, which was finally filed on July 31, 1900, states that Jacob was born in North Carolina and that he had lost his duplicate receipt. Jacob stated that in 1884, he built a framed house and a corn stable, and improved forty acres to a value of $200.00. He had not been absent from the land at all, and he lived with his wife and five grandchildren. On August 4, 1900, Jacob paid $2.70 to the land agent to satisfy the land agent fee. Jacob signed all these documents with an X. The 1900 United States Census also confirmed the family members of Jacob's household.[214]

Two witnesses were required to complete the homestead proof, testimony of witnesses, so Columbus F. Shannon and Edgar A. Smith completed the forms on July 31, 1900, answering similar questions about the improvements on the land and the period of Jacob's residence on the land.

On August 4, 1900, James Hill, register, provided Jacob with Final Certificate no. 15305, which states "that on presentation of this certificate to the commissioner of the general land office, the said Jacob Ramsey shall be entitled to a patent on the tract of land above described."

But Jacob did not present the certificate to the commissioner as directed to make the final proof on March 20, 1901. An affidavit on March 23, 1901, documented that "he failed to make his final proof for which he received Final Certificate no. 15305 through ignorance of the law, requiring him to make final proof within the statutory period that he is an unlettered man, unable to read and write and failed to inform himself of the duties required of him about this claim....He prays that the patent be granted him upon the filing of this affidavit."

One can only imagine how Jacob and Leanna were affected by this notification. The land represented their hopes and dreams for a better life. They had lived on the land for seventeen years, raising their children and grandchildren there. They were some of the founding members of Little Hope Missionary Baptist Church near their land in Toomsuba and were regarded as leaders in their community.[215] Jacob's multiple attempts to complete the proving-up process had not yet led to him gaining title to the land. His inability to read appeared to play a role in his understanding of the land patent process. On October 1, 1901, seventeen years after Jacob's initial land claim, he was finally granted the land patent.

Despite their challenging experience with the federal land patent process, Jacob and Leanna went on to acquire several other pieces of property through private land transactions.

One other interesting fact is revealed in the November 28, 1890, affidavit. Jacob swears that he did not serve for ninety days or more in the army or navy of the United States during the "War of the Rebellion." Often, I had imagined Jacob as a strong, fearless man fighting for the Union for his and his family's freedom, but I was never successful in finding proof. To my disappointment, the land application process confirmed that Jacob did not serve in the Union military, but he swore he did not take up arms against the United States, an eligibility requirement for making the land claim. There were no Civil War records for Jacob Ramsey that could give more genealogical information about Jacob before he gained his freedom.

Based on family Bible records, Jacob died on February 13, 1909.[216] After Leanna died on August 4, 1915, all of the land was divided among the ten adult children, passing along the legacy of independence, financial stability, control over self and respect.[217] However, over the years, all of Jacob's land holdings have been sold or lost due to nonpayment of taxes, as many in the family migrated north. This is disheartening, knowing how Jacob struggled for two decades to meet the requirements for his final land patent.

CONTRIBUTOR: *Jonnie Ramsey Brown descends from Jacob Ramsey, her paternal great-grandfather. A genealogist since 1994, Jonnie compiled and published multiple stories in 2017 about her maternal family titled "Horne, Halsell, Holsey Family Stories: 3 Generations After Emancipation."*

WILLIAM "WILLIE" OR "BOSS" RAMSEY

By Jonnie Ramsey Brown

William Ramsey. *Courtesy of Jonnie Ramsey Brown.*

William "Willie/Boss" Ramsey, my paternal grandfather and the youngest son of Jacob and Leanna Ramsey, was born on December 25, 1880, in Lauderdale County, Mississippi.

According to Boss's only son and my father, Alfred Alphonso Ramsey, William was called "Boss" because everyone in the community respected him. Everyone, Black and white, held Boss in extremely high esteem. My father recalls that when he was hopping trains in the 1930s to visit relatives around the country, he was allowed to sit in the engine car while hobos riding the rails rode in boxcars. Daddy was afforded this special treatment because everyone knew he was Boss's boy.

Boss was an entrepreneur. He constructed many of the homes in Toomsuba and some churches in the area. By Toomsuba standards, he was considered well-off and was one of the first residents to own an automobile. Boss quickly filled a community need by establishing his version of today's Uber; he would give residents rides into Meridian, the county seat of Lauderdale County. This ride service transformed an all-day, twelve-mile trip on treacherous dirt roads by horse or oxen and buggy into a ride that was completed in less than an hour. During the hot and humid summers, the ride service evolved into a necessity. Still another one of Boss's business ventures was that of a private money lender. My father, as a little boy, recalled how Boss would loan money to family and friends and collect weekly payments when in Meridian.

Like his father, Jacob, Boss also homesteaded land in Toomsuba, Lauderdale County, Mississippi. But unlike Jacob, who had many difficulties and took additional years to finalize his land patent, Boss systemically accomplished all the patent requirements in a very timely manner. On January 2, 1903, Boss's application was officially filed at the Jackson, Mississippi Land Office—no. 38313, for 40.01 acres—the northeastern quarter of the southeast quarter of section 19, township 7N, range 18E of the Choctaw principal meridian.

Boss paid the six-dollar fee and signed this document with an X. On all other land documents, Boss signed his signature. Willie Ramsey is the name shown on all the land documents.[218] A notice for publication indicating Boss's intention to make final commutation proof in support of his claim, Homestead Entry no. 38313, appeared in the *Meridian Sun* for five consecutive weeks, beginning on March 23, 1907, and ending on April 21, 1907.

The four neighbors whose names were provided as potential witnesses for the final proof were George Smith, E. A. Smith, Bill Howell and Dave Bramlett, all from Toomsuba, Mississippi.

Boss made the following statements in his final homestead proof, taken before Mr. S.B. Watts, U.S. commissioner at Meridian, Mississippi, on April 26, 1907:

- Stated that he was twenty-seven years old, resided in Toomsuba, Mississippi, and was born in Mississippi.
- Confirmed the description of the land.
- Confirmed he was the same person who filed the original homestead application on January 2, 1903.
- Stated that in January 1903, the improvements made consisted of a three-room frame house with brick chimney, corncrib, smokehouse, fowl house, well, cotton house and stable, for a total value of $500.
- Stated that he lived with his wife and two children.
- Confirmed that he had not been absent from the land since making settlement.
- Stated that he raised crops for five seasons on about fifteen acres.
- Confirmed the claim was not within the limits of an incorporated town or used for a trade or business.

- Described the land as ordinary farming, sandy land, most valuable for farming.
- Confirmed that there are no indications of coal, salines or minerals of any kind on the land.
- Confirmed that he never made any other homestead entry.
- Confirmed he never sold, conveyed or mortgaged any portion of the land.

George Smith, sixty-five, and Bill Howell, fifty-six, were the two witnesses who appeared in person with Boss at the final proof. They gave similar responses to the same questions.

Boss then signed the final affidavit required of homestead claimants and paid $1.60 in commissions and fees at the final proof. His homestead was approved on April 30, 1907.

On September 27, 1907, Willie Ramsey received his land patent, Final Certificate no. 20127.[219]

Ramsey suddenly died intestate on June 25, 1933.[220] His wife, Delia McPherson Ramsey, continued to live on the land until her death on January 24, 1957.[221] My father managed the property in the twenty years after Mother Delia's death, renting it out to tenants and paying taxes. My father and mother, Alfred and Catherine Horne Ramsey, had migrated to Detroit, Michigan, in the late 1930s and then to Los Angeles, California, in the early 1950s, joining millions of other Black Americans who left the South during the Great Migration for better economic opportunities.

Boss had verbally stated on many occasions that he wanted his son—my father—to inherit his land. In the late 1970s, Mother Delia's descendants from prior relationships attempted to settle the legal ownership of the land, trying to cut my father out of his lawful share by claiming he was illegitimate and therefore could not inherit from his father. The ownership of the land was eventually resolved by all parties, as they agreed that my father should receive a 50-percent undivided interest in the land at the time of Boss's death, and the remaining undivided 50-percent interest was given to Mother Delia's descendants. The Lauderdale Chancery Court filed a petition for letters of administration and prayer to waive inventory and appraisal on November 7, 1977, which details the relevant family relationships and this settlement.[222] This is an extraordinarily important legal and genealogical document because it discusses the familial relationships of three generations of the Ramsey and McPherson families.

When my father despondently shared with me the history of Boss's homestead and the division of the land, I encouraged him to buy back his father's land that was in the hands of distant relatives. Over ten years, my father and I were able to acquire 100 percent interest in the original forty acres.

The ownership of Boss's land remains with our Ramsey family today. The younger generations have been educated about the fascinating story behind Boss's land and have been charged with preserving our legacy by keeping the property in the family forever.

CONTRIBUTOR: *Jonnie Ramsey Brown descends from William Ramsey, her paternal grandfather.*

JAMES RIELY (RILEY)

By Norma B. Hall

I became interested in genealogical research after having a conversation with my mother, who shared that her great-great-grandfather Van Riley acquired his land through a land grant. Based on my research, it turned out to be land acquired under the Homestead Act of May 20, 1862. The land continues to be owned by the Van Riley family in Amite County, Mississippi.

James Riely (Riley) filed his homestead land application, no. 15034, at the land office in Jackson, Mississippi, on July 1, 1884, for 165.16 acres of land in Dayton, Amite County, Mississippi, and was awarded his land patent, no. 5803, on March 19, 1891.

James Riely (Riley), on January 25, 1879, married Martha Jenkins from Amite County. He first settled on the property with his family on November 15, 1883, constructing a dwelling house with a kitchen, and he cleared and fenced four acres of land. Eight months later, on July 1, 1884, he filed his claim, signing with an X, swearing that he was the head of his family, over the age of twenty-one and a citizen of the United States.

He lived continuously on the property for five years and cultivated the land. His homestead affidavit described the land as ordinary agricultural land, hilly with about 140 acres of timber. James built a home out of pine poles; it consisted of two rooms, one front room and one back room, and a galley kitchen in the front. He also built a crib for corn, a smokehouse and a

James Riely and his wife. *Courtesy of Norma B. Hall.*

cotton house. He cleared about twenty acres of fenced land and had fifteen acres under cultivation. It was all worth about $200.

In the homestead testimony, James was asked, "Have you voted since establishing residence on the land?" He stated that he voted at the Talbert Precinct, Amite County, Mississippi, since he became of age.

Marshall Johnson and Samuel Johnson were witnesses for James Riely's homestead claim. Mr. Marshall Johnson (forty), a self-employed farmer, attested that he had known James Riley for fourteen years and that he lived in Gloster, Amite County, about five miles from where James resided. He saw the improvements (fencing, fields and buildings) on the farm. Mr. Samuel Johnson (thirty) was also a self-employed farmer living in Dayton, Amite County, and lived three miles from James Riely's farm. He had known him for seven years and could attest to the improvements, such as the cutting of timber and the construction of an eighteen-by-twenty-five-foot dwelling and a shed room on his farm. Samuel Johnson was the brother-in-law of James Riely's (Riley) wife, Martha, and married her sister Laura Jenkins on January 10, 1884.

After five years of marriage, James and Martha had four children, Sarah, Minnie, Susanna and Estelle, as noted in the 1900 U.S. census. As the cultivation of James Riely's (Riley) farm grew, so did his family—from

Van Riley, the brother of James Riley. *Courtesy of Norma B. Hall.*

four children to six additional children, as noted in the 1910 census (Mary, Eunice, Ida William M., Jeanette and James S.). James's eighty-year-old grandmother, Margret Anderson, also resided with him. By 1920, James was a widower, and his children had moved away, except for his two sons William M. and James S. However, James still owned his farm. James Riley died in 1928 in Amite County at the age of seventy-one.

According to Wikipedia:

> *The town of Crosby has been known by several names throughout its history. It was first called Dayton in 1800 in honor of its first merchant, David Day. In 1917, the Foster Creek Lumber Company built a large mill here, and the town was renamed Stephenson in honor of the owner of Fred Stephenson. When L.O. Crosby bought the lumber mill in 1934, the town changed its name to Crosby.*

CONTRIBUTOR: *Norma B. Hall is the great-great-grandniece of James Riely (Riley). James Riely (Riley) was the brother of Van Riley, who was Norma's great-great-grandfather.*

ROBERT VEAL

By Alvin Blakes

Robert Veal was born in February 1872 in Woodville, Wilkinson County, Mississippi. He married Betsy Kain, who was born in February 1873 in Woodville. The 1900 U.S. census lists Robert as a farmer residing on land in beat 3, south of Buffalo Creek, with his wife, Betsy, and three children, Sam, Irene and Martha. Robert's parents were Benjamin Veal and Nora Hull, both born into slavery in Woodville.

Robert Veal filed Homestead Application no. 33417 on September 15, 1898, under the Homestead Act of 1862 at the land office in Jackson, Mississippi. He paid twelve dollars for the submission of his application and signed with an X. His claim was for 81.67 acres of land located on the eastern half of the southeast quarter of section 36 in township 3N, range 1W, of the Washington meridian, located in the Upper Buffalo area of Woodville.

Robert built a two-room log house, which included a crib (barn) and a cotton house, in March 1899 and established residency in the house on April 1, 1889. He farmed on twenty-two acres and raised crops for five seasons. The value of the house was around sixty dollars.

There were four witnesses to Robert Veal's claim: J.C. Whetstone, Alex Carter, Willie Gaulden and Henry Burns, all residents of Woodville, Mississippi. Witness Henry Burns was a Woodville homesteader who was granted forty acres on September 28, 1904, in the same section and township as Robert Veal.

Robert's proof of his homestead claim was published in the *Woodville Republican* newspaper for five successive weeks, from April 30 to May 28, 1904.

The homestead office approved his final certificate, no. 18614, on December 24, 1904, and he received his land patent on February 13, 1905. The claim is recorded in vol. 329 at the homestead office. Before this first homestead claim, Robert Veal did not own any land in Woodville.

CONTRIBUTOR: *Alvin Blakes is a descendant of the Veal family of Wilkinson County Mississippi. He is the great-great-great-great-grandson of Robert Veal Sr., who was born in 1805 in Clarksville, Tennessee. Robert's son Benjamin Veal was the father of homesteader Robert Veal.*

VERDAL WILLS

By Luanne Wills-Merrell

As a young girl, I was captivated by a family artifact in my father's possession—Verdal's homestead certificate. My fascination with this piece of paper grew into a curiosity that could not be satisfied. After researching the family's story for fifty years, I was introduced to land records. The number of details that could be gleaned from the land patent application was amazing. For the first time, the Wills family gained insight into the challenges that our ancestors had to overcome in their quest to obtain land. The biggest surprise in the application package was that Verdal had eighty acres, in addition to and adjacent to his homestead. The number of previously unknown details revealed in the application package motivated me to take my first trip to Choctaw County, where I gained additional understanding from courthouse and library records. It is hoped that sharing Verdal's story will encourage and inspire readers to persevere when faced with challenges.

Verdal (pronounced ver-DELL) Wills was born in Mississippi in November 1841.[223] As an enslaved person in the Deep South, the hope of living as a free man who could provide for his own family must have been a remote dream. Although Verdal was born into slavery, he was part of the unique generation of people who began their lives enslaved and found themselves navigating a new landscape after the Civil War—life as free people. Some freedmen stayed on with their enslavers as sharecroppers, but many took their chances trying to make it on their own. They persevered and successfully worked together to establish neighborhoods, communities, businesses and small towns.

Verdal's wife, Missouri, was born in Texas around 1841.[224] Together, they raised several children who were born in Mississippi. Through a combination of the 1870 and 1880 census records and oral family tradition, I found that their household consisted of Ophelia Brantley (born around 1859), Freeman Deen (born around 1862), Langard Deen (born in 1863 and died in 1953), Harriett Columbia "Cloma" Wills (born around 1864), John "Wesley" Wills (born around 1868 and died around 1920), Nathan Wills (born around 1869), Y. Wills (born around 1876) and Tempie Cecelia Wills (born in 1879).

By 1880, Verdal's two oldest sons, Freeman and Langard, had both changed their last names from Deen to Wills, and Langard changed his first name to Lincoln.[225] Then around 1882, they both relocated from Choctaw County, Mississippi, to Lockhart, Caldwell County, Texas.[226] Lincoln Wills learned the importance of land ownership from his father, Verdal. According to Caldwell County, Texas court records, Lincoln became a landowner on December 12, 1890, purchasing lot 6, block 25, of the Byrd Lockhart League in Lockhart, Texas, for one hundred dollars from L.J. Storey.[227] Lincoln passed his father's value of land ownership on to his children, as evidenced by the fact that the Wills family has owned Lincoln's property for more than 130 years and continuously resided on it for over 100 years. Six of Lincoln's nine children were longtime property holders. His son Freeman built a home in Lockhart, Texas, which, so far, has housed six generations of the Wills family. Even Lincoln's daughters adopted their grandfather's high regard for property ownership. Four of the five daughters were able to purchase their own homes on a maid's salary.[228] Verdal's actions positively influenced future generations of his family.

Verdal's determination to acquire land is consistent with the family's motto: "Where there's a Wills, there's a way." The first documentation of Verdal's lengthy homestead journey appears in Homestead Application no. 17025, dated November 30, 1886. The application indicates that Verdal and his family lived on his original eighty-acre farm since 1873. This property was located on the southern half of the southeast quarter of section 26, township 18N, range 9E, which was next to his future homestead.[229]

Two witnesses, thirty-nine-year-old Alex Beverly and a thirty-six-year-old neighbor Andrew Miller, attested that Verdal had cleared twelve acres of timberland and cultivated it for three seasons. They valued the structures that Verdal built on the land—a dwelling, a stable and a crib—at one hundred dollars.[230] An 1833 survey by Burwell T. Edrington, deputy surveyor, refers to the land as hilly timberland consisting of pine and oak. The soil on the south side of the property is referred to as "sandy," while the east property line is described as having an undergrowth of blackjack (a type of small oak) brush.[231]

In 1894, S.B Dobbs, the clerk of the Choctaw County Circuit Court, added a handwritten note to the homestead application file, stating that Verdal was "ignorant of the law not knowing that it required six weeks publication," referring to the requirement to publish his intent to make final proof in support of his claim to the land for six successive weeks. Lem Seawright, the editor of the *Plain Dealer*, a weekly newspaper out of

Ackerman, Mississippi, personally appeared at the courthouse with a copy of Verdal's notice for publication. By proving that Verdal published his intent to claim the homestead in the *Ackerman Plain Dealer* for six successive weeks, from November 24, 1893, to December 29, 1893, Verdal's quest to obtain the homestead was back on track.

On May 11, 1895, Verdal Wills marked a legal document with an X and acquired a homestead (Homestead Certificate no. 8948). The property was described as the northeast quarter of the southeast quarter of section 26, township 18N, range 9E of the Choctaw meridian in Mississippi.[232] Verdal faced numerous challenges in meeting the requirements of the Homestead Act of 1862. One example is cited in Verdal's 1886 Adjoining Farm Homestead Application, which states that he was unable to appear in the Jackson Land Office in person due to the "distance and the want of money."

Verdal Wills lived to see a dream come true. He became the owner of 39.93 acres in or around the historic town of Kenago in Choctaw County, Mississippi. In one generation, Verdal successfully led his family from slavery to freedom, establishing a 120.00-acre farm and a new way of life for future generations of the Wills family.

CONTRIBUTOR: *Luanne Wills-Merrell is the great-great-granddaughter of Verdal.*

SAILOR ALLEN

By Eric Williams and Antionette Harrell

Sailor Allen was born around 1826 in Amite County, Mississippi. According to the 1870 United States census, he was a farm laborer.[233] In 1850 in Amite County, Mississippi, he married Louisa, who was born around 1835 in Kentucky. Sailor and Louisa had two children living in the house, Isadore Allen and Eli Allen.

Sailor submitted his homestead application, no. 4237, on August 1, 1870, at the homestead land office in Jackson, Mississippi.[234] Sailor couldn't write but signed with an X and paid a seven-dollar filing fee.

During the required period as a homesteader, Sailor cleared, plowed and fenced about sixty acres of land. He built one dwelling house, a kitchen, a smokehouse, a corncrib, a cotton house and a shop.

Adam Harmp and Robert Easley served as witnesses as required for final proof to support the claimants testimony. On August 25, 1876, they both attested that they had known Sailor Allen for fifteen years and that he was the head of his family consisting of his wife and one child. Neither witnesses could read or write and signed with an X on the final proof required under the Homestead Act document. This document also stated that the witness and claimant were prevented from physically attending the land office because of great distance and want of means.

On December 9, 1880, Sailor made it to the receiver's office in Jackson, Mississippi, to finish the final proof and pay the two-dollar fee required by law. He was finally granted Homestead Certificate no. 1979 on January 12, 1882, for section 25, in township 2N, range 5E, containing 80.40 acres of land.

According to the 1900 United States census, both of Sailor's parents were from Africa.[235] He and his wife, Louisa, had been married for fifty years. Sailor was still farming at the age of seventy-two, and his home was free of a mortgage. In his household were his nephew Allen Clines and niece Sarah Allen. Sailor also listed Sarah Amacker as a servant. When Sailor died in Amite County, Mississippi, in July 1918, he had a small estate consisting of 190 acres of land.

CONTRIBUTORS: *Eric Williams is a descendant of the Allen family and shared information with Dr. Harrell about his family history. Harrell and Williams spent several days researching the Allen family in the Amite County Courthouse, and they found several land records in the probate inventory.*

EDMUND DOWNS

By Nona Edwards-Thomas, MD

Edmund (Edmun) Downs was born enslaved in 1844, according to the 1880 Louisiana census.[236] His parents and siblings have not been definitively identified. Edmund, through the Freedmen's Bureau of Refugees and Abandon Lands, signed a labor contract with Levy Bacot on the Levy Bacot Plantation in Pike County, Mississippi, on October 12, 1865.[237] Edmund's age on that contract was listed as thirty-five years old, with a birthdate in 1830. Levy Bacot owned 278 acres and was a former sergeant in the Confederate army. It is unknown how long Edmund worked on the labor contract. On August 3, 1870, in the Pike County, Mississippi census, he is enumerated as Edward Downs; it listed him as a farmhand who could not read or write.

Edmond Downs filed his application, no. 4313, on September 12, 1870, for 120 acres of land in Pike County at the land office in Jackson, Hinds County, Mississippi, for a fee of thirteen dollars.

On the final proof document, dated July 31, 1877, J.J. Simmons and Allen Ford were Downs's sworn witnesses. The witnesses, in a single document, stated that Downs was on the land for six years and was the head of a family with five children. He made improvements by building corncribs, stables and other outbuildings. The names of his wife and five children are not given on the document. The 1880 United States census for Pike County enumerated his second wife, Caroline, and five eldest children, Francis, Richard, Annie, Tom and Mary.

Edmund Downs satisfied the requirements for the homestead patent. He received his homestead certificate, no. 919, on June 30, 1881. In the 1881 personal property tax roll, it lists that he owned two horses and seven head of cattle valued at fifty and forty-nine dollars, respectively. The total valuation of his property was ninety-nine dollars.[238] Edmund worked as a farmer and for another individual in the area.

The *Magnolia Gazette* newspaper reported on September 29, 1882, that while Downs was working for Van C. Coney, the boiler of the steam gin and gristmill exploded.[239] The explosion resulted in Edmund receiving multiple injuries, including a dislocation of the right shoulder, the crushing his left elbow and the scalding of his body. Dr. W.M. Wroten, the doctor in attendance, hoped for a full recovery. Despite his injuries, Downs continued to work on his homestead.

Edmund Downs's unexpected death was reported in the *Pascagoula Democratic Star* newspaper on July 21, 1893: "Edmund Down, a wealthy colored man of Magnolia [Mississippi] was waylaid the other night and shot to death."

In the 1900, Pike County, Mississippi census, Downs's wife, Caroline Downs, is enumerated as a widow.[240] Downs's family continued to live on the homesteaded settlement.

CONTRIBUTOR: *Nona L. Edwards-Thomas, MD, is a cousin of the descendants of Edmund Downs. As a family historian, she has been involved in genealogical research for over thirty years.*

CONCLUSION

The information in this book is representative of the content that others will find when they discover a homesteader in their family and order their land entry case files. However, you will need to study the community and the land acquisition process, and sometimes, you will have to examine court records and explore other documents to determine what happened to the land.

While gathering stories, this author discovered numerous descendants from the South; however, individuals throughout the thirty homestead states are also encouraged to search for homesteaders in their families.

The Homestead National Historical Park Service in Beatrice, Nebraska, is a resource and place to share your stories online (https://www.nps.gov/home/learn/historyculture/homesteading-by-the-state.htm).

Individuals should familiarize themselves with the Bureau of Land Management Patent, an online source for searching for land patents. If a patent is found, the next step is to order the land entry case files from the National Archives and Records Administration in Washington, D.C. Some of these records can also be found online at Ancestry.com, Familysearch.org and the Homestead National Historical Park Service website.

The following simple template can be used to evaluate, write and share your family story:

- What is your ancestor's name?

- Where was he/she born? Was he/she or their parents enslaved?

- When did your ancestor settle on the land? The date should be in the land entry papers.

- When did he/she apply for the land? What is the application number?

- Describe the land improvements: for example, acres cleared, house, outhouse, corncrib, furniture and the value of the improvement(s).

- Add any unique information you know about your ancestor. For example: What was his/her occupation?

- Did he/she live in a predominantly Black community?

- Were his/her witnesses also homesteaders? How do you know this?

- Does your family still own the land?

- Did your ancestor donate land for a church or school?

- Please share what's important to you and your family.

- How many individuals lived with him/her on the homestead? Did he/she name them, or do you know their names?

- Add any family information you would like to share from your family's oral history or research.

- Could he/she read and write?

- Did he/she use a signature or an X to sign her/his name?

- Who were the witnesses? Any unique statements made about the settler from the witnesses?

- When did he/she obtain the land patent? What is the land patent number? List the number of acres acquired.

- Add whatever you would like to conclude your story.

- Do you have a photograph or a unique artifact to add to this story?

- Finally, individuals are encouraged to join the Descendants of African American Homesteaders Facebook group.

UNTOLD STORIES OF BLACK HOMESTEADERS IN FLORIDA

Margo Lee Williams and Falan Goff's Black homesteader ancestors were surrounded by other Black landowners in their communities and surrounding counties. What started as retelling the stories of six Black Florida homesteaders has quickly exploded into the discovery of over one hundred Black Florida homesteaders. These Black homesteaders were found in just four counties: Gadsden, Columbia, Levy and Suwannee. We fully expect to learn of many more homesteaders from other counties in the future. The experience of sharing these stories has shown that the Homestead Act of 1862 provided Black families in Florida with an opportunity to own land and provide for their families, even into succeeding generations. It also set the precedent for their descendants to become landowners themselves.

The following list consists of individuals who were identified as Black homesteaders through a search of the Bureau of Land Management's documents, supplemented with census research.[241]

GADSDEN COUNTY

Nelson, Shaw	January 6, 1873
Davis, Rueben	June 24, 1878
Nelson, Frank	January 6, 1873
Nelson, Richard	January 6, 1873
Jordan, Samuel	January 6, 1873

Columbia County

Livingston, Cesar	January 6, 1873
Dallas, George	July 1, 1875
Fleming, Jordan	November 9, 1891
Fleming, Joseph	June 30, 1884
Fleming, Mark	September 24, 1890
Flemming, Anthony	May 20, 1875
Flemming, Sprague	March 10, 1883
Gaines, Gabe	April 9, 1901
Livingston, Thomas	July 2, 1894
Madison, Hannah	January 17, 1902
Pendleton, Edmund	February 1, 1876
Pendleton, Hartwell	July 1, 1875

Levy County

Glenn, William	June 30, 1884
Merchant, Nelson	June 30, 1884
Simonton, Amy	May 25, 1885
Simonton, Jerry	June 30, 1884
Sims, Benjamin	June 30, 1884
Williams, Henry	August 12, 1891
Dexter, William	June 30, 1884
Payne, Richard	January 20, 1882
Anderson, George	November 4, 1886
Brown, Peter	October 25, 1885
Glenn, Quilla	August 13, 1883
Hammond, Abram	August 13, 1883
Jenkins, Paul	May 25, 1885
Sims, Elias	August 13, 1883
Sims, James	March 3, 1890
Edwards, Ransom	June 30, 1884
Hearn, Daniel	August 13, 1883
Speight, White	June 30, 1883
Days, Adam	April 30, 1883
Spikes, Abram	November 20, 1886
Wade, Edmund	June 30, 1884

Davis, Joseph T.   August 1, 1883
Davis, Moses   February 10, 1885
Davis, Jackson   October 15, 1884
Feaster, Sarah   February 10, 1885

SUWANNEE COUNTY

Adams, Amanda (Patentee Bryant,
   Amanda; same woman)   August 9, 1890
Baker, Anthony   August 5, 1890
Brown, Milton   October 13, 1893
Butler, Elijah   May 20, 1875
Dixon, James J   December 26, 1891
Green, Emerline (wife);
   Green, Moses   August 13, 1883
Harris, Eli   May 20, 1875
Davis, Thomas   February 15, 1889
Henderson, Elijah   September 10, 1872
Jackson, Jesse   July 1, 1875
Johnson, Madison   November 30, 1878
Johnson, Ned   June 6, 1892
Jones, Emperor   February 25, 1885
Jones, Harrison   April 27, 1896
Langwood, Righteous   July 1, 1875
Lawson, London   April 30, 1896
Lee, Dempsey   August 5, 1890
Mckinney, Vinie   June 5, 1890
Medlock, William   November 20, 1888
Meeks, Thomas   October 15, 1884
Monday, Green   February 24, 1894
Pompey, Frank   October 22, 1895
Rawls, Milly   June 30, 1883
Ross, Priscilla   June 24, 1878
Stafford, Dennis   October 13, 1893
Stanley, Moses   October 15, 1884
Smith, Elijah   November 4, 1886
Taylor, Joseph   October 15, 1884
Taylor, Shadrack   June 26, 1889

Thomas, Jesse	December 19, 1885
Thomas, Jessee	June 30, 1884
Timmons, Joseph	October 1, 1883
Washington, George	April 29, 1882
Washington, George	April 30, 1883
Williams, Randal	October 8, 1894
Wilson, Edward	June 15, 1877

NOTES

Introduction

1. Homestead National Historical Park Services, "Homestead Act."
2. Land Entry Case Files and Related Records, https://www.archives. gov/research/land/land-records: Patents are the legal documents that transferred land ownership from the U.S. government to individuals.

Chapter 1

3. *The Sconiers Clan Incorporated Fifth Biennial Session and Reunion of the Descendants of King Dock Alexander I and King Solomon Alexander I,* programme bulletin, July 29 through July 30, 1989. Information derived from the late Charlie Ray Sconiers, the oral griot of the Sconiers Clan Inc., as the only oral document written down concerning Solomon and Dock Sconiers.
4. FamilySearch, "State of Alabama Bureau of Vital Statistics, standard certificate of death, state file no. 7661, entry for Luke Sconyers, April 20, 1920," https://www.familysearch.org/tree/person/memories/K8NW-XTN. Liddie was identified as the mother of Luke, and Solomon was identified as the father of Luke's son, King Sconyers, the informant. The oral history that was passed down identified Liddie Lucious as Luke's mother, as recorded by Keith Sconiers in FamilySearch.

5. Ancestry, "1870 U.S. census, Geneva County, Alabama, population schedule, Township 2, page 607A (handwritten), dwelling 522, family 522, Solomon Sconyers, Mendy Sconiers, Phillis Sconiers, Luke Sconyers, James Scoiners and Tamer Wilkerson," http://www.ancestry.com; NARA microfilm publication M593, 1,761 rolls.

6. Ancestry, "1850 U.S. census, Dale County, Alabama, slave schedule, Allen Sconyers, Slaveholder Southern Division," http://www.ancestry.com; NARA microfilm publication M432, 1,009 rolls. Allen Sconyers's real estate value was $1,400, equivalent to $46,018 in 2020.

7. Alabama Department of Archives and History, "Alabama, voter registration, 1867, Dale County, Election District 5, Precinct 1, Solomon and King Sconyers," http://www.ancestry.com.

8. Ibid.

9. Ibid., 12n.

10. Ancestry, "1880 U.S. census, Geneva County, Alabama, population schedule, Page 635A, E.D.: 078, (handwritten), family 72, Ellen, Sconiers, Luke Sconiers, Bartlet Sconiers, Aaron R. Sconiers, Reuben Sconiers, Lotta Sconiers and Barney Sconiers," http://www.ancestry.com; NARA microfilm publication T9, 1,454 rolls.

11. Ibid., 9.

12. Bureau of Land Management, "Land Patent Search," General Land Office Records, https://glorecords.blm.gov/details/patent/default.aspx?accession=AL4650__.442&docClass=STA&sid=4jdegzry.oaf; Luke Sconyers (Geneva County, Alabama), homestead patent no. 3634.

13. Ibid.

14. Ancestry, "1900 U.S. census, Geneva County, Alabama, population schedule, Campbells, page 2, E.D. 0076, (handwritten), dwelling 40, family 42, Luke Sconyers, Ellen Sconyers, Bartlet Sconyers, Lottie Sconyers, Dan Sconyers, Earley Sconyers, King Sconyers, Eley Sconyers, Solomon Sconyers, Lore Sconyers, Amos Sconyers, Lula Sconyers, Nealie Sconyers and Kattie Sconyers," http://www.ancestry.com; NARA microfilm publication T623, 1,854 rolls.

15. Geneva County, Alabama, deed book A, 385, 453.

16. Ibid., 10n.

17. Keith Sconiers, interview with Charles Wilson, Chicago, Illinois (address maintained by the researcher), May 9, 2020 (notes privately held by interviewer.

18. Ibid., 21n.

19. Ibid.

20. Martha Sconiers Featherston of San Diego, California (addresses maintained by the researcher).

21. Geneva County, Alabama, deed book B-1, 557.

22. *Times Herald*, "Death of an Aged Negro," August 8, 1911, 3, https://www.familysearch.org/tree/person/memories/9N7Y-554.

23. Ancestry, "Alabama, Wills and Probate Records, 1753–1999, Wills, vols. A–B, 1883–1943, Alabama Probate Court (Geneva County)," http://www.ancestry.com; Will of Ellen L. Sconyers, April 21, 1915, recorded by judge of probate, June 3, 19, 1818, 192; Alabama County, District and Probate Courts, images 125, 159, 163.

24. Ancestry, "Ellen L. Sconyers citing Alabama County, District, and Probate Courts," http://www.ancestry.com.

25. Newspapers.com, "Obituary Index, the 1800s: Current Results for Ellen Sconyers," http://www.ancestry.com.

26. Ibid., 256–57.

27. FamilySearch, "Luke Sconyers, April 20, 1920."

28. Ancestry, "Year: *1870*; Census Place: *Township 5, Range 5, Jackson, Mississippi*; Roll: *M593_732*; Page: *439A*," http://www.ancestry.com.

29. FamilySearch, "United States Census, 1880," https://www.familysearch.org/ark:/61903/1:1:M4V3-XQD; William Beard in the household of William Beard, Mobile, Mobile, Alabama, United States, citing enumeration district, sheet, NARA microfilm publication T9, Washington, D.C., National Archives and Records Administration, n.d., FHL microfilm.

30. Original death data: William Beard, May 31, 1939, death certificate no. 11305, roll 3, Mobile, Alabama; the State of Alabama, Mobile, Index of Vital Records for Alabama: Deaths, 1908–1959, Montgomery, AL, State of Alabama Center for Health Statistics, Record Services Division; Find a Grave, https://www.findagrave.com/memorial/69365136/william-beard.

31. FamilySearch, "United States Census, 1870," https://www.familysearch.org/ark:/61903/1:1:MHKZ-KVL.

32. FamilySearch, "Alabama County Marriages, 1809–1950," https://familysearch.org/ark:/61903/1:1:QKZS-NLWC; Warren Law and Betty Jackson, March 9, 1873, citing Henry, Pickens, Alabama, United States, County Probate Courts, Alabama, FHL microfilm 1,288,510.

33. Ancestry, "The U.S. General Land Office Records, 1776–2015," http://www.ancestry.com.

34. FamilySearch, "Census, 1880"; FamilySearch, "Clem Horn, United States Census, 1880," https://www.familysearch.org/ark:/61903/1:1:M4JC-

WHS; Clem Horn, Election Precinct 8, Grant, Coffee, Alabama, United States, NARA microfilm publication T9, Washington, D.C., National Archives and Records Administration, n.d., FHL microfilm.

35. FamilySearch, "Census, 1880"; Bettie Hutchinson in the household of Vandy Hutchinson, Geneva, Geneva, Alabama, United States, citing enumeration district sheet, NARA microfilm publication T9 (Washington, D.C.: National Archives and Records Administration, n.d.), FHL microfilm.

36. M.A. Owen, "Non-Resident Notice," *Elba Clipper*, October 7, 1910, 4, https://www.newspapers.com/image/306845333/.

37. FamilySearch, "United States Census, 1900," https://familysearch.org/ark:/61903/1:1:M98K-GJZ; Cleaveland Horn, Precincts 7–8 St. Paul, Noblin's, Geneva, Alabama, United States, citing enumeration district (ED) 75, sheet 25B, family 512, NARA microfilm publication T623, Washington, D.C., National Archives and Records Administration, 1972, FHL microfilm 1,240,017.

38. Find a Grave, Memorial page for Wiley J. Chancellor (December 4, 1820–November 29, 1893), Find a Grave memorial ID 126875078, citing El Bethel Cemetery, Coffee Springs, Geneva County, Alabama, maintained by Don Atwell (contributor 47043939), https://www.findagrave.com/memorial/126875078/wiley-j-chancellor.

39. Coffee County, Alabama, deed book S, 236–37.

40. FamilySearch, "United States Census, 1910," https://familysearch.org/ark:/61903/1:1:MKQQ-G15; Caroline Homs, Castleberry, Conecuh, Alabama, United States, citing enumeration district (ED) ED 39, sheet 17A, family 27, NARA microfilm publication T624, Washington, D.C., National Archives and Records Administration, 1982, roll 8, FHL microfilm 1,374,021; FamilySearch, "Alabama Deaths, 1908–1974," https://www.familysearch.org/ark:/61903/1:1:J6MC.

41. FamilySearch, "Georgia Deaths, 1928–1943," https://familysearch.org/ark:/61903/1:1:QJXM-YZ5F; Vandy Hutchins in an entry for Daisy Williams, May 19, 1934, citing Blakely, Early, Georgia, Georgia State Archives, Morrow.

42. Almaria James, death certificate (long form), custodian's no. 5063 (1964), early county probate court, Blakely.

43. FamilySearch, "Census, 1900"; Vandy Hutchins, militia districts 1,140, 1,535, Urquhart, Colomokee, Early, Georgia, citing enumeration district (ED) 52, sheet 8A, family 140, NARA microfilm publication T623, Washington, D.C., National Archives and Records Administration, 1972, FHL microfilm 1,240,193.

44. FamilySearch, "Georgia Deaths"; Ella Williams, August 15, 1940, citing Blakely, Early, Georgia, Georgia State Archives, Morrow.
45. FamilySearch, "Georgia, County Voter Registrations, 1856–1941," https://www.familysearch.org/ark:/61903/1:1:4YZG-D1N2.
46. Geneva County, Alabama, deed books U2, 296–97; P2, 266; L2, 670; J2, 422; H, 205.
47. "In Memoriam," *Geneva County Reaper*, November 23, 1928, 1, https://www.newspapers.com/image/535525630/.
48. "Geneva Bank Completes 47 Years in Business," *Geneva County Reaper*, July 20, 1948, 1, https://www.newspapers.com/image/535947475/.
49. Geneva County, Alabama, deed books U2, 296–97; P2, 266; L2, 670; J2, 422; H, 205.
50. FamilySearch, "Georgia, County Voter Registrations, Vandy Hutchins, 1897," www.familysearch.org.
51. FamilySearch, "Census, 1910"; Vandy Hutchins, Urquhart, Early, Georgia, United States, citing enumeration district (ED) ED 83, sheet 8B, family 142, NARA microfilm publication T624, Washington, D.C., National Archives and Records Administration, 1982, roll 184, FHL microfilm 1,374,197.
52. FamilySearch, "Georgia Deaths"; Betty Hutchins, June 1, 1931, citing Early, Georgia, Georgia State Archives, Morrow; FamilySearch, "Georgia Deaths"; Vandy Hutchins, November 29, 1931, citing Early, Georgia, Georgia State Archives, Morrow.
53. Early County, Georgia, deed books, 112, 59.

Chapter 2

54. Arkansas, County Marriages, 1837–1957.
55. 1910 Census, Bradley County, Arkansas, roll T624_44, 10B, enumeration district 0017, FHL microfilm 1,374,057.
56. Arkansas Probate Records, 1817–1979, *Wills v. B. 1860–1933*, 326.
57. Bureau of Freedmen, Refugees and Abandoned Lands, Rations Received, Arkansas Field Office Record, Paraclifta, 29 (1865); Registers of Signatures of Depositors in Branches of the Freedman's Savings and Trust, 1865–1874; Administrator's Bond Volumes A–B, Hempstead County, Arkansas, March 3, 1841, 140-151; Bureau of the Census, Ninth Census of the States, Washington, D.C., Population of the United States in 1870, 21, Sevier County, Arkansas.

58. Inventories and Wills, 1819–1824, Will of John Harpole, Wilson County, Tennessee, November 11, 1820, 90.

59. Ibid.

60. Bureau of the Census, United States, Tenth Census of the States, Washington, D.C., Population of the United States in 1880, 18, sheet 10C, Sevier County, Arkansas.

61. John A. Hopson, interview with Lyle Gibson, Kansas City, KS, February 15, 1990; Elizabeth Gibson, interview with Lyle Gibson, Kansas City, KS, January 1, 1990.

62. Ibid., 66.

63. Ibid., 67.

64. Ibid. After the Civil War, individuals received food and other assistance from the federal government.

65. Bureau of the Census, Tenth Census of the States, Washington, D.C., Population of the United States in 1880, Sevier County, Arkansas, 30, sheet 40C; Bureau of the Census, Twelfth Census of the States, Washington, D.C., Population of the United States in 1900, Sevier County, Arkansas, 184, sheet 11B.

66. Bureau of the Census, Thirteenth Census of the States, Washington, D.C., Population of the United States in 1910, Sevier County, Arkansas, sheet 11B.

67. FamilySearch, "United States, Freedmen's Bureau, Records of Freedmen's Complaints, 1865–1872," https://familysearch.org/ark:/61903/1:1:Q2QR-4KW4; H.C. Pride, July 28, 1865, citing Residence, Arkansas, NARA microfilm publication M1901, Records of the Bureau of Refugees, Freedmen and Abandoned Lands, 1861–1880, RG 105, Washington, D.C., National Archives and Records Administration, n.d., roll 18, FHL microfilm 2,424,770.

68. FamilySearch, "United States Census, 1870"; 1870, census place: Clear Creek, Sevier, Arkansas; roll: M593_64; page: 259A.

69. Land entry papers of Irving Bass, Bureau of Land Management, document 7,536, misc. no. 15000 AR NO S/N Accession Nr. AR2760_.348, document type: State Volume Patent State Arkansas Issue, January 23, 1899.

70. Ibid.

71. Author's conversation in 1977 with Ellen Bass Walton, who shared her memories about her childhood in Horatio, Arkansas.

72. Ibid.

Chapter 3

73. FamilySearch, "Florida Marriages, 1830–1993, Alex Gainer and Francis Gainer, 1874; FHL microfilm 1,940,234," https://familysearch.org/ark:/61903/1:1:23HY-63R.

74. Florida Memory, "Suwannee County, Florida, Voter Registration Rolls, 1867–1868, Precinct 3 (Live Oak): Aleck Gainer," https://www.floridamemory.com/items/show/290830.

75. "Pensacola and Georgia Railroad Company to Alexander Gainer and George Manker," in Suwannee County, Florida, deed book B, 131 (copy in possession of the author).

76. Ancestry, "1870 U.S. Federal Census, Subdivision 9, Suwannee County, Florida; Alex Gainer, Head. NARA Roll: M593-133; 693B; image 522; Family History Library Film: 545632," https://www.ancestry.com/imageviewer/collections/7163/images/4263359_00522?pId=3484546.

77. FamilySearch, "Florida Marriages."

78. Alexander Gainer, Homestead Final Certificate 1,236, June 14, 1877, Bureau of Land Management, General Land Office Records, Washington, D.C. (copy in the possession of the author).

79. Alexander Gainer, Homestead Application 5,609, May 11, 1872, Bureau of Land Management, General Land Office Records, Washington, D.C. (copy in the possession of the author).

80. Alexander Gainer, Homestead Application Affidavit, May 11, 1872, Homestead Application 5,609, Bureau of Land Management, General Land Office Records, Washington, D.C. (copy in the possession of the author).

81. Linc Wilson, receiver, Receiver's Receipt 5609, Alexander Gainer, Homestead Application 5609, June 14, 1872, Bureau of Land Management, General Land Office Records, Washington, D.C. (copy in the possession of the author).

82. Caleb Simpkins and Robert Allen, witness affidavit, June 1, 1877, Alexander Gainer, Homestead Application 5609, Bureau of Land Management, General Land Office Records, Washington, D.C. (copy in the possession of the author).

83. Ibid.

84. Alexander Gainer, Homestead Final Affidavit, June 14, 1877, Homestead Application on 5609, Bureau of Land Management, General Land Office Records, Washington, D.C. (copy in the possession of the author).

85. John Varnum, receiver, Final Receiver's Receipt, June 14, 1877, Homestead Application 5609, Bureau of Land Management, General Land Office Records, Washington, D.C. (copy in the possession of the author); Alexander Gainer, Homestead Final Certificate 1236, Homestead Application 5609, Bureau of Land Management, General Land Office Records, Washington, D.C. (copy in the possession of the author).

86. Land Office Card, Gainesville, Florida, Alexander Gainer, Homestead Application 5609, Bureau of Land Management, General Land Office Records, Washington, D.C. (copy in the possession of the author).

87. "Alexander Gainer to M.M. Blackburn," in Suwannee County, Florida, deed book J, 289 (copy in the possession of the author).

88. "Alex Gainer and Frances Gainer to Corra Manker," in Suwannee County, Florida, deed book K, 136 (copy in the possession of the author).

89. "Frances Gainer to James Moore and C.J. Manker," in Suwannee County, Florida, deed book S, 436 (copy in the possession of the author).

90. "Ellen Williams and Carry Manker to Jesse Manker, April 10, 1901," in Suwannee County, Florida deed book (copy in the possession of the author); "Ellen Williams and Carry Manker to Mamie Edwards, March 27, 1911," in Suwannee County, Florida deed book (copy in the possession of the author).

91. The story of Simon "Sim" Bell's Homestead application is available on the National Park Service Homestead National Historic Park's "Black Homesteaders Project" website: https://www.nps.gov/people/sim-bell.htm.

92. Year: 1900, census place: Chattahoochee, Gadsden, Florida, 15, enumeration district: 0037, FHL microfilm: 124,016.

93. Ancestry, "Eliza Kilcrease, Dodd, Jordan R, et. al., Early American Marriages: Florida to 1850, see also in the Gadsden County, Florida, U.S., Compiled Marriages, 1851–1875," https://search.ancestry.com/cgi-bin/sse.dll?dbid=4019&h=3510&indiv=try&o_vc=Record:OtherRecord&rhSource=8784.

94. Bureau of Land Management, General Land Office Records, Washington, D.C., Federal Land Patents, State Volumes, Homestead Application 5620, Sim Bell Testimony, December 16, 1878.

95. Ibid.

96. Ancestry, "Sim Bell, United States, Bureau of Land Management, Florida Pre-1908 Homestead and Cash Entry Patents, General Land Office Automated Records Project, 1993, See also United States, Bureau of Land Management, Florida, U.S., Homestead and Cash Entry

Patents, Pre-1908," https://search.ancestry.com/cgi-bin/sse.dll?dbi d=2071&h=33020&indiv=try&o_vc=Record:OtherRecord&rhSour ce=6742.

97. Ancestry, "Year: 1880; census place: Precinct 9, Gadsden, Florida; roll: 128; 264B; enumeration district: 056," https://www.ancestry.com/ discoveryui-content/view/4497908:6742.

98. Ancestry, "Schedules of the Florida State Census of 1885; National Archives Microfilm Publication M845, 13 rolls; Records of the Bureau of the Census, record group 29; National Archives, Washington, D.C.," https://search.ancestry.com/cgi-bin/sse.dll?dbid=7605&h=146394&indiv =try&o_vc=Record:OtherRecord&rhSource=6742.

99. Bureau of Land Management, General Land Office Records, Washington, D.C., Federal Land Patents, State Volumes, Homestead Application 5620, Sim Bell Testimony, December 16, 1878.

100. Ancestry, "Year: 1880; census place: Precinct 9, Gadsden, Florida."

101. Personal knowledge and information from Maud Woods Humphries.

102. The story of Randel Farnell's homestead application is available on the National Park Service Homestead National Historic Park's "Black Homesteaders Project" website: https://www.nps.gov/people/randel-farnell.htm.

103. Death Certificate, Randel Farnell, October 27, 1928, Florida File 16,372, Department of Health and Rehabilitation Services, Bureau of Vital Statistics (copy in possession of the author).

104. Ancestry, "Final Distribution of the Estate of Elisha Farnell, in Georgia, U.S., Wills and Probate Records, 1742–1992, image: 377," https://www.ancestry.com/imageviewer/collections/8635/ images/005778373_00377; Ancestry, "Onslow County, North Carolina Land Grant 1,773, Elisha Farnell, August 15, 1800, North Carolina, U.S., Land Grant Files, 1693–1960," https://www.ancestry.com/ imageviewer/collections/60621/images/44173_354511-01173?ssrc =pt&treeid=66453873&personid=36156402732&hintid=&usePUB =true&usePUBJs=true&_ga=2.62566633.479788417.1639854993- 842894759.1623784412&_gac=1.24164424.1636000892. Cj0KCQjw5oiMBhDtARIsAJi0qk0tlfEdxH7R5hI16k2H1fwjkO 4pMqCVW8Mikaeq6tMgDfIMNfvvaIQaAoWlEALw_wcB&pId= 97477; Scott B. Thompson Sr., "The Founding of Laurens County," *Pieces of Our Past: Laurens County Court House, Dublin, Georgia*, http:// dublinlaurenscountygeorgia.blogspot.com/2015/04/the-founding-of-laurens-county.html?m=1; "Representatives and Senators from Pulaski

County Since It Was Created 1808," in *History of Pulaski County, Georgia: Official History*, compiled by the Hawkinsville chapter of the Daughters of the American Revolution (Atlanta, GA: Press of Walter W. Brown Publishing Company), 1935; Ancestry, "Elisha Farnell, Representative, 1818 and 1819, Elisha Farnell, Senator," https://www.ancestry.com/discoveryui-content/view/65:22837?ssrc=pt&tid=66453873&pid=36156402732.

105. Ancestry, "Inventory and Appraisement of the Estate of Elisha Farnell, December 22, 1823, Georgia, U.S., Wills and Probate Records, 1742–1992," https://www.ancestry.com/imageviewer/collections/8635/images/005778373_00390.

106. Ancestry, "Final Distribution of the Estate of Elisha Farnell."

107. Ancestry, "1850 U.S. Federal Census, Free Schedule, District 1, Hamilton, Florida; James Farnell, Head, NARA Roll: M432-58, 226B," https://www.ancestry.com/imageviewer/collections/8054/images/4193083-00445?pId=18449607.

108. Ancestry, "U.S. Civil War Soldier Records and Profiles, 1861–1865, James Farnell, enlisted: March 14, 1862; wounded: September 17, 1862; died: October 14, 1862," https://www.ancestry.com/discoveryui-content/view/425480:1555?ssrc=pt&tid=66453873&pid=36156400968.

109. Ancestry, "1870 U.S. Federal Census, Columbia County, Florida, Randel Farnell, Head, NARA Roll: M593-128, 396A, Family History Library Film: 545627," https://www.ancestry.com/discoveryui-content/view/2270561:7163?ssrc=pt&tid=66453873&pid=36156388330.

110. Ancestry, "1870 U.S. Federal Census, Subdivision 9, Suwannee County, Florida, William Jacobs, Head, NARA Roll: M593-133, 686A, Family History Library Film: 545632," https://www.ancestry.com/imageviewer/collections/7163/images/4263359_00507?pId=448439.

111. Bureau of Land Management, General Land Office Records, Washington D.C., Federal Land Patents, State Volumes, Randel Farnell, Homestead Application 5647, Patent 4776 (copies in the possession of the author); Ancestry, "U.S., General Land Office Records, 1776–2015, Randel Farnell, Final Certificate," https://www.ancestry.com/imageviewer/collections/1246/images/RHUSA2007B_FL0750-00489?pId=259832.

112. Ibid.

113. Ibid.

114. Ancestry, "Florida, County Marriages, 1823–1982, Joe Jacobs and Addie Magee, married: April 29, 1899, Suwannee County," https://www.ancestry.com/discoveryui-content/view/1608271:61369?ssrc=pt&tid=66453873&pid=36246085580.

115. Ancestry, "1880 U.S. Federal Census, Precinct 1, Suwannee County, Florida, Randel Farnell, Head, NARA Roll: 132; 282C, enumeration district: 145," https://www.ancestry.com/discoveryui-content/view/38857191:6742?ssrc=pt&tid=66453873&pid=36156388330.

116. Bureau of Land Management, General Land Office Records, Washington, D.C., Federal Land Patents, State Volumes, Homestead Application 5647, Randel Farnell Testimony, October 4, 1884.

117. Ancestry, "1910 U.S. Federal Census, Live Oak, Suwannee County, Florida, Randell Farnell, Head, Street: Anderson Street, NARA Roll: T624-168, 18A; enumeration district: 0148; FHL microfilm: 1374181," https://www.ancestry.com/discoveryui-content/view/3103816:7884.

118. Private conversation between Granddaughter Lute Williams Mann and Margo Lee Williams.

119. FamilySearch, "Florida, County Marriages, 1830–1957, Randall Farnel and Priscilla Vickers, December 26, 1907, FHL microfilm 963,513, "https://familysearch.org/ark:/61903/1:1:FW3S-1B7.

120. Death Certificate, Randel Farnell, date of death: October 27, 1928, Florida File 16,372, Department of Health and Rehabilitation Services, Bureau of Vital Statistics (copy in Possession of the author).

121. Ancestry, "Florida Death Index, 1877–1998, Prescilla V Farnell, died: December 1967," https://search.ancestry.com/cgi-bin/sse.dll?dbid=7338&h=1168904&indiv=try&o_vc=Record:OtherRecord&rhSource=60525.

122. Personal knowledge.

123. Henry McGehee's homestead story first appeared on the National Park Service's "Black Homesteaders Project" webpage: https://www.nps.gov/people/henry-mcgehee.htm; National Park Service, "Randel Farnell," https://www.nps.gov/people/randel-farnell.htm.

124. Ancestry, "Florida, County Marriage Records, 1823–1982, Marriage of Henry McGehee and Jane Smiley, May 13, 1866, Suwannee County," https://www.ancestry.com/discoveryui-content/view/1192757:61369?ssrc=pt&tid=66453873&pid=36246088141.

125. Voter Registration Rolls, 1867–68, Suwannee County, Florida; Florida Memory, "Henry McGee," https://www.floridamemory.com/items/show/290909; Ancestry, "article title," https://www.ancestry.com/discoveryui-content/view/9483:70876.

126. Bureau of Land Management, General Land Office Records, Washington, D.C., Federal Land Patents, State Volumes, Henry McGehee, Homestead Application 4169, patent 1225 (copies in the possession of the author); National Park Service, "Henry McGehee Homestead Case File, Florida," https://www.nps.gov/media/photo/gallery.htm?pg=6995234&id=488A6BB3-1E59-41C7-BF8C-D237FD274BF2.

127. National Park Service, "Final Proof, May 7, 1877, Henry McGehee Homestead Case File, Florida," https://www.nps.gov/media/photo/gallery.htm?pg=6995234&id=488A6BB3-1E59-41C7-BF8C-D237FD274BF2.

128. National Park Service, "Homestead Receipt, 1869 (1), Henry McGehee Homestead Case File, Florida," https://www.nps.gov/media/photo/gallery.htm?pg=6995234&id=488A6BB3-1E59-41C7-BF8C-D237FD274BF2.

129. National Park Service, "Letter, November 1876, 1–3, Henry McGehee Homestead Case File, Florida," https://www.nps.gov/media/photo/gallery.htm?pg=6995234&id=488A6BB3-1E59-41C7-BF8C-D237FD274BF2.

130. National Park Service, "Grant for Final Proof, Henry McGehee Homestead Case File, Florida," https://www.nps.gov/media/photo/gallery.htm?pg=6995234&id=488A6BB3-1E59-41C7-BF8C-D237FD274BF2.

131. National Park Service, "Final Affidavit, in Photo Gallery: Henry McGehee Homestead Case File, Florida," https://www.nps.gov/media/photo/gallery.htm?pg=6995234&id=488A6BB3-1E59-41C7-BF8C-D237FD274BF2.

132. National Park Service, "Final Certificate 1225, Henry McGehee Homestead Case File, Florida," https://www.nps.gov/media/photo/gallery.htm?pg=6995234&id=488A6BB3-1E59-41C7-BF8C-D237FD274BF2.

133. Ancestry, "1880 U.S. Federal Census, Precinct 1, Suwannee County, Florida, Henry McGee, Head, NARA Roll: 132, 292C, enumeration district: 145," https://www.ancestry.com/discoveryui-content/view/6015060:6742.

134. Bureau of Land Management, General Land Office Records; Washington D.C., USA; *Federal Land Patents, State Volumes*. Randel Farnell, Homestead Application 5647, Patent 4776. Copies in the possession of the Author. Witness testimony, William Evans, and Henry McGHee.

135. Ancestry, "Marriages, Joe Jacobs and Addie Magee"; Ancestry, "1870 U.S. Federal Census, Subdivision 9."

136. Ancestry, "1910 U.S. Federal Census, Precinct 2, Suwannee County, Florida, Joseph Jacobs, Head, Henry McGhee, father-in-Law, NARA Roll: T624-168; 28B, enumeration district: 0148, FHL microfilm: 1374181," https://www.ancestry.com/imageviewer/collections/7884/images/31111_4327454-00108?pId=3104126.

137. FamilySearch, "Census, 1900"; FamilySearch, "Florida Deaths, 1877–1939," https://familysearch.org/ark:/61903/1:1:FP4D-S9J.

138. FamilySearch, "United States Census, 1870"; FamilySearch, "Census, 1880"; Stephen McCaskill in household of John McCaskill, Walton, Florida, United States, citing enumeration district, NARA microfilm publication T9, Washington, D.C., National Archives and Records Administration, FHL microfilm.

139. FamilySearch, "Florida Deaths"; FamilySearch, "Florida Marriages"; Stephen McCaskill and Emma Houston, 1891, citing marriage, Walton, Florida, United States, citing multiple county clerks of court, Florida, FHL microfilm 931,219.

140. FamilySearch, "Census, 1900".

141. Ancestry, "U.S., General Land Office Records, 1776–2015," www.ancestry.com.

142. Ibid.

143. FamilySearch, "Census, 1910"; Stephen McCaskill, Freeport, Walton, Florida, United States, citing enumeration district (ED) 110, sheet 6B, family 119, NARA microfilm publication T624, Washington, D.C., National Archives and Records Administration, 1982, roll 169; FHL microfilm 1,374,182.

144. FamilySearch, "Florida Marriages, 1837–1974," https://familysearch.org/ark:/61903/1:1:FWM1-NQR.

145. FamilySearch, "United States Census, 1920," https://www.familysearch.org/ark:/61903/1:1:MJ8B-Y4L; FamilySearch, "United States Census, 1930," https://www.familysearch.org/ark:/61903/1:1:X4DV-LSS; Dealyer M Drinkard in household of Nicholas Drinkard, Newark (Districts 1-250), Essex, New Jersey, United States, citing enumeration district (ED) 34, sheet 1B, line 55, family 13, NARA microfilm publication T626, Washington, D.C., National Archives and Records Administration, 2002, roll 1333; FHL microfilm 2,341,068.

146. FamilySearch, "Census, 1930"; James Drinkard, Newark (Districts 1-250), Essex, New Jersey, United States, citing enumeration district

(ED) 34, sheet 2A, line 1, family 25, NARA microfilm publication T626, Washington, D.C., National Archives and Records Administration, 2002, roll 1333, FHL microfilm 2,341,068.

147. FamilySearch, "New York, New York City Marriage Records, 1829–1940," https://familysearch.org/ark:/61903/1:1:247V-812; Jim Drinkard and Emma Mcskell, April 10, 1926, citing marriage, Manhattan, New York, New York, New York City Municipal Archives, FHL microfilm 1,643,631.

148. Ibid.; FamilySearch, "Florida Marriages"; Stephen McCaskill and Millie Campbell, 1920, citing Marriage, Walton, Florida, United States, citing multiple County Clerks of Court, Florida, FHL microfilm 931,223.

149. FamilySearch, "Census, 1930"; Stephen McCaskill, Freeport, Walton, Florida, United States, citing enumeration district (ED).

150. FamilySearch, "United States Census, 1940," https://www.familysearch.org/ark:/61903/1:1:VTZS-C9J; Steve McCaskil, Freeport, Walton, Florida, United States, citing enumeration district (ED) 66-12, sheet 10A, line 14, family 168, Sixteenth Census of the United States, 1940, NARA digital publication T627, Records of the Bureau of the Census, 1790–2007, RG 29. Washington, D.C., National Archives and Records Administration, 2012, roll 622.

151. FamilySearch, "Florida State Census, 1945," https://familysearch.org/ark:/61903/1:1:MNJM-4J7; Steve Mccaskie, Freeport, Walton, Florida, citing line 39, State Archives, Tallahassee, FHL microfilm 2,425,212.

152. Ancestry, "Bureau of Land Management, General Land Office Records; Washington D.C.; federal land patents, state volumes; U.S., General Land Office Records, 1776–2015," www.Ancestry.com.

153. Ancestry, "Census Place: Goshen Hill, Union, South Carolina; Roll: M593_1510; Page: 419A," www.ancestry.com; Ancestry, "The Church of Jesus Christ of Latter-day Saints," www.ancestry.com; census place: Old Store, Chesterfield, South Carolina; roll: 1225, page: 388A, enumeration district: 008; Ancestry, "1900 United States, Twelfth Census of the United States, 1900," www.ancestry.com; census place: LaCrosse, Alachua, Florida, roll: 165, page: 5, enumeration district: 0002, FHL microfilm: 1240165.

154. State archive, Tallahassee and clerk of courts, various counties; Ancestry, "Tallahassee, Florida, County Marriages, 1823–1982," www.ancestry.com.

155. Find A Grave, "1600s–Current," www.findagrave.com.

Chapter 4

156. Year, 1880; census place: Livingston, Louisiana; roll: 456; 170A; enumeration district: 138. During this census, Charles was living with his mother, and his occupation was that of a farmer and swamper.
157. Calvin Mitchell was married to Rebecca Watson in 1913 in Livingston Parish, Louisiana.
158. Ancestry, "U.S., Freedman's Bank Records, 1865–1874," www.ancestry.com.
159. Peter Batice, Homestead Application 8554 and Land Patent 5410 for 80.00 acres, issued date: June 28, 1895, in Maurepas, LA, Bureau of Land Management.
160. Homestead Land Entry File 9844 from the National Archives and Records Administration, Washington, D.C.
161. Ovide Alexis, Homestead Application 10396 and Land Patent 5308 for 160 acres, issued date: January 22, 1895, in Maurepas, LA, Bureau of Land Management; Gumersindo A. Vidal, Homestead Application 8553 and Land Patent 5409 for 80 acres, issue date June 28, 1895, in Maurepas, LA, Bureau of Land Management.
162. Excerpts of this story were previously published in *La Créole, A Journal of Creole History and Genealogy* 11, no. 1 (October 26, 2018); A family Bible dated 1895, with names and dates recorded, is in the possession of Bernice A. Bennett.
163. Freedmen's Bureau of Refugees and Abandoned Land, record group 105, roll 36.
164. Ancestry, "1870 U.S. Census, St. Helena Parish (Louisiana) pop. schedule, house no. 28, fam. no. 28, Mary Johnson household," www.ancestry.com.
165. Ancestry, "1880 U.S. Census, St. Helena (Louisiana) pop. schedule, house no. 194, family. no. 194, Peter Clark household," www.ancestry.com; Matrimonial Bond (Peter Clark to Rebecca Youngblood), State of Louisiana, Parish of St. Helena, Sixth Judicial Court, July 15, 1874.
166. Ancestry, "1880 U.S. Census, Peter Clark household."
167. Year: 1870; Census Place: Ward 3, St. Helena, Louisiana; roll: M593_529, 97A; Ancestry, "1880 U.S. Census pop. schedule, Livingston Parish, Louisiana; household no. 221, fam no. 221," www.ancestry.com.
168. Parish of Livingston, State of Louisiana, succession of Thomas Youngblood, opposition to the appointment of Robert M. Benefield, administrator, box 11, filed December 4, 1882.

169. Original Homestead Land Entry Papers, application 9590, certificate 5887, National Archives and Records Administration, Washington, D.C.

170. Ancestry, "1880 U.S. Census, Livingston Parish."

171. "Notice for Publication," *Southland*, October 17, 1894.

172. 1900 U.S. Census; census place: Maurepas, Livingston, Louisiana; roll T623_568; 2A; enumeration district: 60.

173. Certificate of death, State of Louisiana, Secretary of State, Division of Archives, Orleans Death Indices, 1909–1917, vol. 146, 874.

174. Homestead Case File for Frank Thompson's land application, no. 13841; Patent no. 4814, NARA, Washington, D.C.

175. Detail of George Gauld's 1778 *A Plan of the Coast of Part of West Florida and Louisiana*, Adapted 2022, D.M. Franklin.

176. Year: 1910; census place: Police Jury Ward 4, Washington, Louisiana; roll: T624_534; 1B; enumeration district: 0129; FHL microfilm: 1,374,547.

177. Homestead Land Entry File 7,570 was obtained from the National Archives and Records Administration, Washington, D.C.

178. Year: 1900; census place: Police Jury Ward 4, Washington, Louisiana; 9; enumeration district: 0099; FHL microfilm: 1240585.

179. Ibid.

180. Homestead land patent no. 12085, Bureau of Land Management, 158.62 acres.

181. Genesis 23:7–20; 47:13–26; Job 1:1; 42:12–15, New World Translation of the Holy Scriptures (New York: Watch Tower Bible and Tract Society of Pennsylvania, 2013).

182. Document obtained in July 2007 at the courthouse located in Greensburg, St. Helena Parish, Louisiana.

183. Bureau of the Census, Ninth Census of the States, Washington, D.C., Population of the United States in 1870, 11, sheet 124, Tangipahoa Parish, Louisiana.

184. Bureau of the Census, Tenth Census of the States, Washington, D.C., Population of the United States in 1880, 9, sheet 445A, Tangipahoa Parish, Louisiana.

185. Bureau of the Census, Twelfth Census of the States, Washington, D.C., Population of the United States in 1900, 181, sheet 9B, Tangipahoa Parish, Louisiana.

186. Louisiana deaths 1850–1875 and 1894–1960, Kentwood, Tangipahoa, Louisiana, certificate 6415, State Archives, Baton Rouge, FHL microfilm 2,364,414.

187. Civil War Invalid and Widows Pension 97,1991 and certificate, Company G, Tenth Regiment of United States Colored Heavy Artillery Volunteers, National Archives and Records Administration.

188. Year: 1880; census place: First Ward, St. Helena, Louisiana; roll: 468; 380D; enumeration district: 152.

189. Homestead Land Entry Papers for John Turner, application 21150 and certificate 12327, National Archives and Records Administration, Washington, D.C.

190. Ibid.

Chapter 5

191. United States 1880 Census National Archives micropublication, T9 roll 662, Heritage Quest 348A, sheets 33 and 34, Pike County, Mississippi, enumeration district (ED) 37, supervisor district (SD) 3, dwelling 274, family 276.

192. United States 1900 Census National Archives micropublication, T9 roll 663, Heritage Quest 40A, sheet 8, Pike County, Mississippi, enumeration district (ED) 105, supervisor district (SD) 7, dwelling 112, family 113.

193. Ibid.

194. Mississippi marriages 1800–1911, marriage records, colored, vol. 1–2, 1872–1890.

195. Mississippi, Homestead and Cash Entry Patents, Pre-1908.

196. Mississippi State Archives various records, 1820–1951, Pike County tax rolls, 1881–1886, box 3,752.

197. 1920 U.S. Census, West Park, Cuyahoga County, Ohio.

198. Ancestry, "1880 United States Federal Census, MS, Franklin, 143, 47 of 60," https://www.ancestry.com/imageviewer/collections/6742/images/42411988-00052?pid=41164024.

199. Franklin County Index; Marriage Index 1825–1949; Colored Marriages, Book 4; page 282; Source: FamilySearch.org.

200. U.S. World War I draft registration cards, 1917–1918.

201. Find a Grave, "Freewoods Cemetery, Franklin County, Mississippi, USA (April 6, 1874–March 20, 1938)," https://www.findagrave.com/memorial/113229782/daniel-gibson.

202. Department of the Interior, Bureau of Pensions, Washington, D.C., claimant's statement in compliance with circular no. 62 of the Pension Office, statement by Peter Hunt (1892), reproduced by the National Archives, 2.

203. Mississippi, Freedmen's Bureau Office Records, 1865–1872, Natchez (southern district of Mississippi), roll 35, Registry of Freedmen, August–October 1865, image 42 of 77.

204. Ancestry, "*U.S., Federal Census Mortality Schedules Index, 1850–1880,*" www.ancestry.com; Year: 1870; census place: Franklin, Mississippi; roll: M593_729; 82B; image: 168; Family History Library Film: 552,228.

205. Department of the Interior, Bureau of Pensions, Washington, D.C, claimant's statement in compliance with circular no. 62 of the Pension Office, statement by Peter Hunt (1892), reproduced by the National Archives, 2.

206. Ancestry, "1850 United States Federal Census, Henry Hunt, Mississippi, Amite, 65 of 116," www.ancestry.com; 1860 U.S. census, slave schedules for Henry Hunt, Mississippi, Franklin, 24.

207. Bureau of Pensions, certificate no. 1129794, record of enlistment from January 1864–May 13, 1866, dated August 4, 1911.

208. Department of the Interior, Bureau of Pensions, Washington, D.C., file of Peter Hunt, certificate 1129794.

209. U.S. Civil War Pension Index, general index to pension files, 1861–1934, roll no. 232, 4,084–416.

210. Department of the Interior, Bureau of Pensions, Washington, D.C, statement of January 4, 1907, by Henry Hunt (HFM) in the U.S. Pension Office files, filed June 1, 1904, to December 21, 1907, stamped January 11, 1907.

211. Death Certificate Index 1912–1934, Bureau of Vital Statistics, Mississippi, Hunt, Peter-Franklin-c-12222Jc16734-15.

212. African American Civil War, https://afroamcivilwar.org.

213. The patent details for Jacob Ramsey's homestead application can be found at: https://glorecords.blm.gov/details/patent/default.aspx?access ion=MS2660__.393&docClass=STA&sid=esqoz3yn.a3y.

214. Ancestry, "1900 United States Federal Census, place: Hurricane Creek, Lauderdale, MS, roll T623 815; 310B, enumeration district: 28," http://search.ancestry.com/cgi-bin/sse.dll?db=1900usfedcen&h=28010 938&ti=0&indiv=try&gss=pt.

215. Facebook, "Little Hope Missionary Baptist Church," https://www.facebook.com/littlehopetoomsuba/, Little Hope Missionary Baptist Church in Toomsuba, Mississippi, was founded in 1879 by Reverend Benjamin F. Whitehead, Brother Jacob Ramsey, Sister Leanna Ramsey and others. In 1887, Brother Jake and Sister Leana donated a one-acre plot, where the church now stands.

216. Deaths, Thomas Lamar family Bible (American Bible Society, 1881), In 2021, the original Bible was in the possession of Bernice Lamar Herring of Akron, Ohio. The Thomas Lamar family Bible was passed from Thomas Lamar to his son Allen Lamar. Upon Allen Lamar's death, it was passed on to his niece Bernice Lamar Herring.

217. Leanna Ramsey death record, August 1915, state file no. 15688, Mississippi State Department of Health Vital Records (a certified copy is in the possession of great-granddaughter Jonnie Ramsey Brown).

218. Willie Ramsey, Mississippi, United States, pre-1908 general land entry files, Homestead Act, section 19, Township 7-N, Range 18-E, homestead final certificate 20,127, Jackson, Mississippi Land Office, records of the Bureau of Land Management, Washington, D.C., National Archives and Records Administration (copies are also in the possession of granddaughter Jonnie Ramsey Brown).

219. The patent details for Willie Ramsey's homestead application can be found at: https://glorecords.blm.gov/details/patent/default. aspx?accession=0661-363&docClass=MV&sid=cpvungmm.4ct#patent DetailsTabIndex=0.

220. Will Ramsey's death record, June 25, 1933, state file no. 8970, Mississippi State Board of Health, Bureau of Vital Records (a certified copy is in the possession of granddaughter Jonnie Ramsey Brown).

221. Delia Ramsey's death record, January 24, 1957, state file no. 914, Mississippi State Department of Health Vital Records (a certified copy is in the possession of granddaughter Jonnie Ramsey Brown).

222. Lauderdale Chancery Court petition for letters of administration and prayer to waive inventory and appraisal filed November 7, 1977, in the matter of the estate of Delia McPhearson Ramsey, deceased, petitioner: Tommie Lee Hinson Warfield, case no. E-186, minute book no. 220, 646 (copies of the petition are also in the possession of Jonnie Ramsey Brown).

223. Choctaw County, Mississippi Census Records, 1900.

224. Choctaw County, Mississippi Census Records, 1870.

225. Issaquena County, Mississippi Census Records, 1880; Choctaw County, Mississippi Census Records, 1880.

226. Dee Azadian, ed., *Earth Has No Sorrow* (n.p.: Voluntary Action Center, 1977).

227. Caldwell County Texas Deed Records, vol. 19, 520.

228. Luanne Wills-Merrell, "The Wills Family of Lockhart, Texas," in *Plum Creek Almanac*, vol. 38 (n.p., 2020).

229. Choctaw County, Mississippi Land Deed Index for section 26, township 18N, range 9.

230. Homestead Land Entry papers, application no. 17025, NARA, Washington, D.C.

231. Choctaw County, Mississippi 1833 Land Survey for township 18, range 9.

232. Verdal Wills, Homestead Certificate no. 8948, NARA, Washington, D.C.

233. Year: 1870; census place: between Osyka and Greensburg R., Amite, Mississippi; roll: M593_721; 495A.

234. Homestead Land Entry papers application no. 4237, NARA, Washington, D.C.

235. Year: 1900; census place: Beat 5, Amite, Mississippi; 6; enumeration district: 0028; FHL microfilm: 1,240,799.

236. Edmond Downs household, 1880 U.S. Census, Pike County, Mississippi, population schedule, SD 3, ED 37, 29, dwelling 240, family 241.

237. National Archives in Washington, D.C.; Records of the Assistant Commissioner for the State of Mississippi, Bureau of Refugees, Freedmen and Abandoned Lands, 1865–1869; NARA series no. M826; NARA reel no. 48; NARA record group 105; NARA record group name: Records of the Bureau of Refugees, Freedmen and Abandoned Lands, 1861–1880; collection title: United States Freedmen's Bureau Labor Contracts Indenture and Apprenticeship Records, 1865–1872, roll: 48.

238. Mississippi State Archives, various records, 1820–1951, Pike County tax rolls, 1881–1886, box 3,752.

239. "A Serious Explosion" *Magnolia* (MS) *Gazette*, September 29, 1882, Content of the news story detailing the injury of Edmond Downs.

240. Year: 1900; census place: Beat 1, Pike, Mississippi; 8; enumeration district: 0105; FHL microfilm: 1,240,825.

Untold Stories of Black Homesteaders in Florida

241. U.S. Department of Interior, Bureau of Land Management, General Land Office Records, https://glorecords.blm.gov/search/.

SELECTED BIBLIOGRAPHY

Websites

HistoryGeo.com. https://www.historygeo.com/. A family history software service for linking old maps and land records to your genealogy research.

Homestead National Historical Park Services. "Black Homesteaders, Black Homesteading in America." https://www.nps.gov/home/black-homesteading-in-america.htm.

———. "The Homestead Act of 1862." https://www.nps.gov/home/homestead-act-of-1862.htm.

National Archives. "Land Entry Case Files and Related Records, NARA." https://www.archives.gov/research/land/land-records. (Patents are the legal documents that transferred land ownership from the U.S. government to individuals.)

Thomas, Nona Edwards. *Brumfield Genealogy and Other Branches and Trees.* https://brumfieldgenealogy.blogspot.com.

Publications

Bennett, Bernice Alexander. *Tracing Their Steps: A Memoir, My Journey to Find Granddaddy's Land in Livingston Parish, Louisiana.* Palmyra, VA: Shortwood Press, 2019.

Blassingame, John W. *Black New Orleans, 1860–1880.* Chicago: University of Chicago Press, 1973.

Edwards, Richard, PhD, Mikal Brotnov Eckstrom, PhD, and Jacob K. Friefeld, PhD. "Black Homesteaders in the Great Plains." Historic Resources Study for the National Park Services, Center for the Great Plains Studies University of Nebraska, December 1, 2019.

Gray, Joyceann. *Proofing the Claim, Beginning of Black Homesteading*. Blurb, Reischling Press, 2022.

Hawkins, Kenneth. Research of the land entry files from the General Land Office, record group 49, reference information paper 114, National Archives and Records Administration, Washington, D.C., revised 2009.

Marchand, Sidney. *Flight of a Century 1800–1900*. Donaldsonville, LA, 1936.

———. *The Story of Ascension Parish*. Baton Rouge, LA: J.E. Ortlieb Printing Co., 1931.

McCall, Keith Dennis. "Prairie, Property, and Promise: Black Migrants and Farmers in Kansas, 1860–1885." Master's thesis, University of Mississippi, 2013. https://egrove.olemiss.edu/etd/1205.

Micheaux, Oscar. *The Homesteader, A Novel*. Sioux City, IA: Western Book Supply Company, 1917.

Mitchell, Thomas W. "'Destabilizing the Normalization of Rural Black Land Loss: A Critical Role for Legal Empiricism,' 2005 Wis. L. Rev. 557 (2005)." https://scholarship.law.tamu.edu/facscholar/.

Oubre, Claude F. "Forty Acres and a Mule: Louisiana and the Southern Homestead Act." *Louisiana History: The Journal of the Louisiana of the Louisiana Historical Association* 17, no. 2 (Spring 1976): 143–57.

Painter, Nell Irvin. *Exodusters: Black Migration to Kansas After Reconstruction*. New York: Norton Paperback, 1992.

Patterson, Ruth Polk. *The Seed of Sally Good'n: A Black Family of Arkansas, 1833–1953*. Lexington, KY: University Press of Kentucky, 1996.

Poret, Ory G. *History of Land Titles in the State of Louisiana*. Baton Rouge: State of Louisiana, Division of Administration, State Land Office, 1972.

Records of the Field Offices for the State of Louisiana, Bureau of Refugees, Freedmen and Abandoned Lands, 1863–1872, record group 105, Washington, D.C., National Archives and Records Administration.

USDA. "Black Farmers in America, 1865–2000: The Pursuit of Independent Farming and the Role of Cooperatives." RBS Research Report 194.

Vincent, Charles, ed. "The African American Experience in Louisiana: Part B: From the Civil War to Jim Crow." In *The Louisiana Purchase Bicentennial Series in Louisiana History*, vol. 9. Lafayette: Center for Louisiana Studies, University of Louisiana at Lafayette, 2000.

ABOUT THE AUTHOR

ernice Alexander Bennett is an award-winning author, genealogist, nationally recognized guest speaker, storyteller, and producer-host of the popular *Research at the National Archives and Beyond BlogTalkRadio* program. She was also the first recipient of the Ida B. Wells Service Award, which is given by the Sons and Daughters of the United States Middle Passage, for her dedication to broadcasting stories about enslaved and indentured ancestors of African descent. She also received the Elizabeth Clark-Lewis Afro-American Historical and Genealogical Society (AAHGS) Genealogy Award in 2019 for her original research in support of African American genealogy. Bennett is a volunteer with the Homestead National Historical Park Service and has devoted her grassroots skills to identifying and encouraging descendants of Black homesteaders to share their stories. In addition, she is also on the board of directors for the National Genealogical Society and one of the founders and faculty members for the Midwest African American Genealogy Institute.

Bennett, a New Orleans native and current resident of Maryland, enjoyed a thirty-five-year-long career in domestic and international public health. She received an undergraduate degree from Grambling State University and a graduate degree in public health from the University of Michigan.

Her genealogical research centers on Southeast Louisiana and Edgefield and Greenwood Counties, South Carolina. Her South Carolina journey is chronicled in *Our Ancestors, Our Stories*, which won the 2018 International AAHGS Book award for nonfiction short stories. Her second book, *Tracing Their Steps: A Memoir*, received the Phillis Wheatley Literary Award from the Sons and Daughters of the United States Middle Passage in 2019, the International AAHGS Book Award in 2020 for nonfiction short stories and the Next Generations Indie Award in 2021 for the African American nonfiction book category.

Visit us at
www.historypress.com
....